Expanding HORIZONS

by Mark Bjork

The Suzuki-Trained Violinist Grows Up

Alfred Publishing Co., Inc.
16320 Roscoe Blvd., Suite 100
P.O. Box 10003
Van Nuys, CA 91410-0003
alfred.com

Cover Photos: Jerry Taskier

Cover photos courtesy of the New World
Symphony, America's Orchestral Academy,
Michael Tilson Thomas, Artistic Director.

ISBN-10: 0-7390-5109-1
ISBN-13: 978-0-7390-5109-2

CONTENTS

CHAPTER 1
"WHEN WILL THEY BE READY FOR REAL LESSONS?"

Several years ago I received a note from the parent of a 13-year-old student informing me that the boy was now "ready for real work." This particular student had come to me at age 5. During his time with me he had covered a quantity of literature, soloed with three professional orchestras playing major works from the Romantic virtuoso repertoire, and had about half of the Paganini Caprices successfully under his belt by age 13. If he had not been doing "real work" until then, what was he doing?

This situation has repeated itself many times with minor variations. The question, "When will they be ready for real lessons?" is asked all too often by parents of Suzuki-trained students, and sometimes by the students themselves. It reflects a lack of understanding of the true meaning of Suzuki's Talent Education, or Mother Tongue Method. Many still believe that the Suzuki Method somehow differs from traditional teaching in the ultimate result, and that if the student reaches an advanced level and wishes to continue pre-professional studies, he or she will need to go to a "traditional" teacher. Often, the student or parents conjure this idea when they are told by a well-meaning friend or professional musician that the youngster is ready for a traditional violin teacher, or "real lessons." Despite the decades that the Suzuki Method has been successfully practiced, too many people still believe it is a beginner's method, only capable of taking a student so far. This belief is frequently based on the fact that Suzuki students read no music in the beginning stages, whereas in reality, many eventually develop excellent reading skills. Regardless of the method used to teach violin or other instruments, the same skills must eventually be acquired, including reading music. The order in which the skills are learned does not necessarily need to be the same. The aforementioned traditional teacher is usually a fine performer, but may have inadequate experience with young students, or understanding of the new student's background, and/or serious pedagogical training of her own. Even if this transition is successful for the young student, it can be a painful experience if the new, traditional teacher comes from a completely different philosophical point of view from that of the Suzuki Method.

Let us take a moment to examine, once again, what the Suzuki Method is and what the students should accomplish on the journey towards the realization of their goals.

The Suzuki Method is both a philosophy and a methodology. To summarize in the briefest way, the philosophy maintains that musical ability is a matter of the acquisition of skills stimulated by the environment rather than reflecting a genetic predisposition. Suzuki believed that every child could be educated, as evidenced by the universal ability to learn to speak the mother tongue. This profound observation has expanded our expectations and understanding of the level of accomplishment every child can attain. Suzuki did not say that every child could or would develop to the level of an artist. He did, however, continue during his lifetime of work and observations to raise this estimate of the minimum level that every child could achieve. String education has not been the same since, with vast numbers of students reaching levels that were once thought to be the domain of a select few. How has this happened? Teachers and parents have believed in the potential of the child, and applied a carefully-conceived, thoroughly-tested, and constantly-modified methodology. In its proper implementation, the Suzuki Method involves an intensive emphasis on listening, a step-by-step introduction of new skills, and repetition and revision of previously learned repertoire in an environment of positive reinforcement from teachers, parents, and fellow students. This approach to learning is equally appropriate at any level, from the beginner to the mature artist.

At this time, some 40 years after Suzuki's work was first presented outside Japan, comprehensive teacher training programs are in effect in most parts of the world. Teacher trainees study the philosophy and the core curriculum, and are steeped in the careful, step-by-step approach to learning that we have come to associate with Dr. Suzuki's Method. In addition, many of these teachers bring to their Suzuki work their own extensive musical training and advanced skills for playing their instruments. They should be well-qualified to take students to any desired level of study. Many of these teachers have expressed a desire for repertoire suggestions, within the Suzuki philosophy, to use beyond the ten volumes of "Suzuki Violin School" as well as study material for the advancing student's technical development. The purpose of this book is to provide suggestions to tweak the imagination and help teachers expand their horizons in these areas, as well as to discuss some of the related issues specifically relevant to the adolescent violinist who plays at an advanced level. These topics include learning to work alone, developing excellent reading skills, and relating to the greater musical community in school and youth orchestras, summer camps, competitions, and so on. In no way is "Expanding Horizons" intended to be a set method, but rather suggestions gleaned from approaches the author has found to be successful in 40 years of teaching students from 2-year-old beginners to graduate-level performance majors. May it serve to tweak the creativity and imagination and expand horizons!

Here is one last note about content. It goes without saying that a student needs and deserves well-maintained, professional-quality equipment. This is a topic for another book, equally important to philosophy and pedagogy, but one which I shall not cover at this time.

I would like to acknowledge the assistance of a number of people who have helped make this book possible. Thanks to Catherine van Zanten, a participant in a Colorado Suzuki Institute teacher workshop, who suggested the title, "Expanding Horizons." "Because that's what it is," she said. Beatrice Blanc, as my graduate student at the University of Minnesota, helped with the repertoire list. Sam Sandon and Nate Tramm, two of my students, posed the photos taken by Womack Photography and Montzka Photography. I am deeply grateful to Jonathan Reynolds, PhD, MSc, PT of Arts Medicine Minnesota, a physical therapist internationally recognized for his work with performing artists, for his valuable suggestions on "Chapter 19: Are We Setting Our Students up for Pain?" My wife, Nancy, who is a highly-successful string teacher, a former writing teacher, and a Suzuki parent, patiently spent countless hours working on the manuscript to make sure what I put on paper was what I meant to convey. My daughter, Alice, re-typed many chapters. Thanks to my two daughters, Karen and Alice, who helped me experience being a Suzuki Parent! My greatest indebtedness, no doubt, is to my countless students who have, over the years, taught me more than I could have ever taught them.

CHAPTER 2
THE WEANING PROCESS:
PREPARING FOR THE TEEN YEARS

Weaning is a natural and desirable phenomenon, whether it refers to weaning from the breast, or in the parent-child relationship in the Suzuki Triangle. As the student grows it is natural that he or she will desire more independence in many ways, including in the musical working relationship. This can be a difficult time for the student if the appropriate groundwork for this process has not been laid. It can also be an extremely upsetting period for the parent who has made an enormous investment of time, energy, emotion, and money. If handled correctly, however, this process of letting go can become less of a trauma and more of a continuing step in the overall progression of learning and growing. The roles do change, but can, nevertheless, remain rewarding and enjoyable.

As a teacher, my ultimate goal is to make myself obsolete. I hope over the course of time I will be able to give my students the tools to teach themselves. My goal is to provide them with the necessary technical equipment, a sense of musical style learned from their environment, good practice skills, and the curiosity and motivation to continue to explore the vast world of music available to them. This is not to say that I have nothing more to offer them after high school, or that they do not often go on to additional music study elsewhere. I simply want them to be prepared to function independently as mature musicians. I also deeply value keeping in touch with my students as they travel along their lives' paths; no matter how large or small a part music plays in each life, I hope it will at least remain a presence.

In the discussion of this important topic at a summer institute in the 1990s, Suzuki piano teacher Francoise Pierridon warned that the Suzuki Triangle could easily become the "Suzuki trap." This dynamic is something we should avoid. Over the years a wonderful working relationship develops between the Suzuki child, parent, and teacher. That is how we have been able to get to this level! Strong bonds have developed and they will not be broken, but these parent-child bonds will probably be tested, as they no doubt will in other areas of the parent-child relationship. We expect this as parents and must prepare for and deal with it.

In this regard, I often think of my very first student in the Suzuki program at the MacPhail Center for Music in Minneapolis. This boy began lessons at about 6 years of age. He and his mother developed an excellent working relationship and, according to his mother, a great relationship beyond the music. This is just the kind of thing we hope for. This mother even expressed to me that she was sorry the Suzuki Method was not around for her older children—she felt that she and her youngest son shared something special that she could not share with her other children. Mother and son attended lessons together, practiced together at home, and attended group lessons and recitals.

All was well until one day when the boy, now age 12, announced he wanted to attend lessons alone! He was then on his own and, quite frankly, not prepared for this moment. He sometimes experienced difficulty as he learned the skills necessary to practice on his own, but his parents remained supportive and we all weathered the storm. Suddenly, during his junior year of high school, the young man announced that he would now like his mother to visit his lessons again. She worked in downtown Minneapolis where the school was located, and easily arranged to meet her son after work for his lesson at my studio. He visibly enjoyed her presence as he played. What he never saw, because of the arrangement of furniture in my studio, was that the moment his mother came in and sat down after a busy day at work, she promptly fell asleep and napped for the duration of the lesson, no doubt soothed and comforted by her son's beautiful music. Needless to say, I never told!

Instead of a smooth transition like this, an attitude problem may emerge in the pre-teen or early teen years. One day a student might turn to the parent and say, "I don't want to do this any more. It was never my idea in the first place. This was always your thing!" In this case we can point out to the student what has been accomplished: the good times with friends at group lessons, and so on. However, if we are honest, we must agree that the student is correct. After all, if this child began study at the early age of three or four, the decision was ultimately the parent's. The child may have heard other children playing instruments and seen that they were enjoying themselves, but in reality it is the parent who must decide to spend countless hours driving to lessons and related activities, taking notes and practicing at home, not to mention shouldering the emotional and financial investment! We do not have an honest rebuttal for this child. Beginning Suzuki study at a young age is a parental decision made with the best interest of the child in mind as parents consider general music study and the Suzuki experience, in particular, to be something truly valuable and worthy of many sacrifices.

We can prepare in advance for this possible moment. The key is to be sure that the student has already taken ownership in the music experience. As parents and teachers we must be sure that he or she is "hooked." The Suzuki environment offers many opportunities to accomplish this if we take advantage of them. The most effective encouragement is positive peer pressure — we know how susceptible youngsters are to this. The many group activities that begin with the first lesson are modified as the student grows so they continue to be age-appropriate. The group games that are so much fun at age four are not such fun at 14. Adapting the social and musical activities so they are geared to the growing student helps to cement friendships, many of which probably originate in the first lessons and have the potential to last a lifetime.

Working against the student's sense of ownership is the potential danger inherent in the Suzuki Method: placing the student in a position that is passive. For example, the parent decides that the child will begin instruction. The first lessons usually begin with the parent playing rather than the child, so that the child is primarily an observer of the parent-teacher relationship. Later, when the child begins to play, the teacher still often gears much of the instruction to the parent in order to make him or her an effective home teacher. The child watches and responds only when told. At home the parent is necessary as a practice supervisor and director. Again, the ideal Suzuki child does just as he or she is instructed. Sometimes a recorded accompaniment is played and the student dutifully follows; the recorded pianist, after all, is not able to adjust in any way to the child. At group lessons, the young player follows the group that usually includes stronger, more advanced students. This is one of the biggest motivators of students of the Suzuki Method. At the solo recital, the teacher usually secures an accompanist who is intimately familiar with the string student repertoire being performed, and who often leads the novice performer through insecure moments on stage. In all of these situations, the student can easily assume a role that is passive.

As an antidote to this potential passivity, I suggest we look for ways to get the student actively involved. Will this not help him or her to take ownership in the music and build skills that will be available when he or she needs to begin to work alone?

Involve the child from an early age in some decision-making aspects of practice. Offer choices to the beginning student. "Would you like to practice now or after dinner?" "Would you like to practice in the family room or in the kitchen while I wash the dishes?" "Would you like to play 'Lightly Row' first, or 'Go Tell Aunt Rhody'?" "Do you think you should repeat that section 15 times or would 20 times be better?" Note that these questions should not enable a negative response from the student, and any of the student's choices should fit into a well-planned practice routine. The key is to involve students rather than simply direct them.

As the student matures, the options change and the questions take on a different nature. I suggest that analyses become a major part of the mature student's practice, resulting in more active student participation.

The following is an example of a typical practice session.

When the child finishes a piece, the parent asks, "How do you think you played?" After the child responds, the parent asks, "What do you think could improve?" The parent then asks,

"What did your teacher suggest to take care of that problem?" "How can you fix that?" The parent continues with engaging questions. "How many times does that need to be repeated?" "How secure does that feel now?" "Are you ready to try that section all at once?" Obviously, the choices presented must consider the child's ability, age, and stage of development. Remember that a pleasant attitude with ample positive reinforcement is just as important for the mature student as it is in the beginning stages. Also, while beginning to offer choices, maintain sensitivity to your child when he or she tires of responsibility and needs you to take over. After all, maturity does not happen all at once!

Independence at the lesson is another area in which a gradual, natural process should be thoughtfully conceived by the teacher and parent together. "Communication" is the key word, just as it has been throughout the teaching/learning experience. First of all, the teacher and parent must remember that the lesson is ultimately for the child, not for the parent. The teacher should make it a point to speak directly to the child, rather than the parent. The parent should be careful to wait to ask questions until the teacher is finished working with the student. Such care helps avoid the classic moment in which the teacher corrects the student, who then turns to the parent and says, "You never had me do that." "You told me the wrong way!" The student must begin to accept some responsibility.

The physical arrangement of the studio can promote student independence. When a young child begins lessons in the typical Suzuki situation, the parent is seated as close to the child as possible so he or she, as the home teacher, can see clearly. Naturally, the teacher is also close to the child. As the student matures, both the teacher and the parent should move farther away allowing the student distance, giving the teacher a more complete view, and creating a gradual parent-child separation. This is a subtle but significant factor in avoiding a physical environment that can be smothering.

All good Suzuki parents have learned to take notes. This is how they function well as home teachers even though they are usually inexperienced with the instruments their children are learning to play. I apply a gradual transfer of this note-taking responsibility to the child. First, around age 10, I ask the student to begin taking a duplicate set of notes during the lesson. Since the student is usually untrained to assume this responsibility completely, I ask him or her to write down what I want the student to do at home. I stop along the way during the lesson to allow time to write. I encourage writing down whatever helps the memory, adding that complete sentences and correct spelling are unnecessary. I look over shoulders to see if what the student thinks I said is what I think I said. The results are interesting and often hilarious! This is a good reality check for me as the teacher, for I am frequently reminded just how specific my instructions need to be for the student to have an effective week of practice at home. Many times in the past I have sent students home with the instructions, "Fix that!" "Clean that up!" Worse yet, I have said, "Obviously you know what needs to be done." I now realize that the nature of the problem is not always obvious to the student. Why should it be? Even if a student has the experience necessary to identify a problem, he or she often lacks the ability to fix it. It takes a long time to be able to relate current and past problems, and to remember how the previous problems were solved. Little by little, students' notes assume a greater role in the overall learning process, while parents' notes assume a lesser one.

Other devices that help achieve student independence are the tape recorder and mini-disk recorder. Teachers usually have recorders in their studios, and students and parents often make good use of it to help them remember lessons. The young student can take over the responsibility of bringing a blank cassette or disk, putting it in the machine, and turning it on. To facilitate this change I announce that I am too busy, and if the student desires a recording he or she should start the tape. I do not think for a moment that these tapes are always listened to every week at home! I do know, however, that recordings sometimes solve arguments between the parent and the child about what was said in the lesson. In addition, many families now own a video camera which can be even more useful in capturing a lesson. In this case, too, some of the set-up responsibility can be transferred from the parent to the maturing child.

At some point after consultation between parent and teacher, the student may have an occasional or partial lesson alone. The parent may drop the young musician at the lesson, and then run a quick errand or take an extra-long time parking the car so the student can begin the lesson alone. Gradually, the parent might arrive later and later, sometimes not attending at all. The idea is to make the process gradual, rather than an abrupt change for which the child is not prepared.

Sometimes the teacher must initiate the aforementioned process. I once suggested to the mother of one of my students that she might occasionally send her child alone for a lesson. She declined, responding that she very much enjoyed attending the lessons. Next, I suggested that she might like to run an occasional errand during the lesson, but she answered that she had plenty of time to take care of such things while her daughter was in school. I finally hinted that, since the school was so close to downtown, she might want to do a bit of shopping. She didn't like to shop either! In the end, I was direct and outlined a schedule whereby the mother would come to three out of four, then two out of four, and finally one out of four lessons. Eventually the mother was to come for an occasional visit only when her daughter invited her. This mother had been very involved, worked well with her daughter, and enjoyed the whole experience immensely. Stepping back was extremely difficult for the mother, but it was necessary for the student to learn to work effectively and accept responsibility. When it was all over, the mother and I enjoyed many good laughs over this period in her child's development.

This gradual approach should be used at home and in the lesson. Following consultation with the teacher, the child should begin by doing a small part of the practice routine alone. This small part could include lesson review, a reading assignment, or repetitions of a passage to be perfected. Obviously the student should not begin this process with new material or a particularly difficult spot. Eventually the parent's role might be to simply check up on the work the student has done alone. Later still, the parent might be called upon to listen to the new piece the child has prepared entirely on his or her own. The sensitive parent will know when to give a suggestion and when to remain silent, letting the teacher deal with an inaccuracy that may have been obvious all week! Although remaining silent may be difficult for the parent as a skilled home teacher, part of the maturing process requires that young Susie or Johnny learn to accept responsibility for work done incorrectly.

Try using a practice process with steps that the young player can easily identify and learn to use independently. I suggest this five-step diagnostic process:

1. Play a piece and ask if anything needs to be improved. (The Examination)

2. After identifying the problem, decide how to correct it. (The Diagnosis)

3. Do the necessary work to affect a "cure." (The Medicine)

4. Play the piece again to see if the cure has been achieved. (The Check-Up Exam)

5. Decide if the cure needs to be continued at the next practice in order to maintain excellent health. (The Maintenance Plan)

At first, the parent and child can follow all five steps in this process together at home. In the early stages of independence the student may handle one or two steps alone. Over time, the parent can bow out of the process completely.

The clue to success here is a gradual transfer of responsibility— "cold turkey" simply does not work. We should build on the security and confidence the child has developed during the years of working closely with a parent in a Suzuki environment. Sometimes in a moment of extreme frustration, the home teacher will throw up his or her hands and say, "I'm through! You're on your own. I can do nothing with you!" The child may say, "I want to do this myself. I don't want you around anymore!" Neither really means these words, but we should be honest with ourselves. We are all human, these times do happen, and we sometimes say things we later regret. If the seeds of independence have already been sown using some of the techniques outlined here, this stage of the parent-child relationship can go more smoothly. The change that takes place during this transition to independence will not destroy the musical relationship that the two generations share. Remember, no matter how independent the student becomes in lessons and practice, parental support and reinforcement are always needed.

CHAPTER 3
MOTIVATING THE OLDER STUDENT
Group Lessons, Tours, Chamber Music, Summer Opportunities

The Suzuki environment offers many extraordinary motivational opportunities. From the beginning the student should see his or her parent playing and enjoying the violin. While many teachers think of this as a time for the parent to learn the instrument to be a more effective home teacher, Dr. Suzuki viewed it as a motivational opportunity. The child, seeing the parent play and have a good time, imitates the parent. When the child begins to participate, he or she is surrounded by other children who are also playing the violin. His or her private lesson includes observation of more advanced childrens' lessons. Then there are group lessons and recitals to attend, which are vital to this approach to learning. For many there are workshops on weekends and institutes during the summer, with long-lasting friendships developing along the way. Families able to take advantage of these offerings will see their children progress and develop, often at rapid rates. All in all, the child grows up in an enriched environment — music becomes a way of life.

By the time a student reaches the advanced level, it might be tempting to take this motivation for granted. Some things may change as the student grows older, but others, such as motivation, may simply take a different form. While watching his or her parent struggle through "Twinkle Variations" may no longer motivate the teenager, the social opportunities that music offers may be even more motivating to the older student.

The group lessons most Suzuki programs offer as integral parts of the learning experience are helpful in early stages, and can continue to be so for the advanced student. However, these lessons should be tailored to the specific ages and needs of the students involved. It is exciting and highly motivating for young children to be in a group with older, more advanced pupils. The young ones hear older students play advanced repertoire with beautiful tones and more solid techniques. Young students are inspired by what they hear and often say, "I want to play like that someday." This inspiration is a major motivator for the young player.

While older students may, on one level, enjoy being role models, they should not be expected to serve in this capacity repeatedly or indefinitely. We can ask them to play with the beginning students and expect them to agree to a reasonable number of requests. Of course, some of the older students will be particularly agreeable and will want to participate every time. Large group concerts are a tradition in most Suzuki programs and some older students find them very enjoyable. They may be attracted to the opportunity to be in the back row at last with the "big kids!" I recall telling a high school senior about a huge group concert at an upcoming state festival that he and his friend were welcome to attend. Although I said I would understand if they did not want to participate, to my surprise his response was, "What?" "Miss that concert with all the little kids? That's the most fun thing we do all year!" They did play, much to the delight of the younger children, and were fine role models. However, not all 18-year-old boys will find such delight in playing the familiar pieces one more time, or may be unwilling to admit they enjoy it. Such reluctance is normal, and we should be sensitive to our older students. After all, how many times over how many years can we realistically expect them to be excited about playing the Eccles "Sonata"?

Group lessons for skilled students can still be tailored into a valuable experience. At least some group sessions should be limited to the most advanced players, and possibly to the older, more advanced students. The peer group that is so important throughout the Suzuki experience is even more important for teenagers, for whom the social aspects of any activity become a major attraction. Students enjoy being with their friends; when they share the common bond of music-making over the years, the experience is even more enjoyable. The wise teacher will allow students the opportunity to socialize at group lessons, and also at specially organized, age-specific activities. These may be special concerts played and/or attended by the students, social events, and trips. Any kind of trip is great for bonding, and food is always an attraction. All of these activities highlight for students the joy and importance of playing an instrument.

The important thing to remember is that the older, more advanced students need the opportunity to be with each other exclusively, regardless of playing level. Grouping students by age, rather than by playing level, may be difficult for younger virtuosi and their parents to understand. This practice, however, can be highly significant to teenage students, especially those who are less advanced and may feel intimidated by young, accomplished players. An age-specific event does not mean the end of joint opportunities for all students. It does mean that time will be reserved for older players by themselves. After all, they have provided a role model and motivation for younger players for years. They deserve some reward.

Repertoire for the advanced-group lesson offers the chance for unlimited creativity. Not only are there pieces in the later volumes of "Suzuki Violin School" that work well for unison playing, but the vast array of violin literature and the world of music beyond provide endless possibilities. To benefit from this, however, the teacher must be willing to explore what is available in many genres, and often seek out or create special arrangements. Many solo pieces will work as arrangements, as well as the wealth of material for two, three, and four violins found in many libraries and publishers' lists. In addition, many genres beyond the standard repertoire have provided a source for group arrangements — those published by Thomas Wermuth and Michael McLean are excellent. Other avenues to explore include fiddling, mariachi, and numerous books recently published for strolling string groups. Holidays offer yet another source of inspiration and possibility. A mix of styles might be just the thing to capture the student imagination.

If violas, cellos, and a double bass are available, another world opens up. The repertoire for chamber ensembles and string orchestra is vast. Moreover, a string orchestra provides an easy transition from the traditional Suzuki group lesson — many skills studied in group lessons also characterize an orchestra rehearsal. Large Suzuki programs often include cellists and violists. If violists are unavailable, explore the possibility of securing several violas, preferably on the small side, and let the violinists take turns learning a second instrument. After a bit of explanation about alto clef — no faking, please — and a little experimentation, the violinists will be on their way to a new and rewarding musical experience. Who knows? A select student may develop a love for this rich instrument. Several of my students have done just that and now boast auspicious careers as professional violists! Perhaps the large program has bass players. If not, consult with the nearest private bass teacher for a student of similar age and ability who would enjoy and benefit from a string orchestra experience. If limited to school and youth orchestra experiences, students may never reap the benefits of all-string repertoire. School and youth orchestras rarely devote a majority of time to all-string repertoire because that would leave the woodwinds, brass, and percussion players with nothing to do. In an exclusively string ensemble, students can truly hear themselves play and develop wonderful ensemble skills. In addition, Baroque and Classical repertoire, from which a great deal of string-orchestra literature comes, provides terrific preparation for larger symphonic works and chamber music.

This brings us to chamber ensembles: duos, trios, quartets, quintets, sextets, and larger groups for which many composers have written some of their finest compositions. It brings great pleasure to devoted chamber players; most string players admit that they would rather play chamber music than almost any other literature. Once exposed to the repertoire and having developed the needed skills, most young players admit the same preference. For the teacher, matching the players and scheduling the rehearsals and coaching sessions is a huge challenge, but well worth the effort. When a young musician takes responsibility for his or her own part, real growth occurs. It becomes necessary to have impeccable intonation, beautiful tone, strong rhythm, a sense of style, and mastery of a wide range of bow strokes. Once confidence has been built, the chamber player begins to realize the importance and joy of playing an individual part.

Teachers and coaches, of course, should be very careful choosing literature for beginning chamber music players. Parts must be undemanding to enable the novice player to concentrate on requisite ensemble skills, rather than only managing the notes. In fact, this attention to choice is crucial in all ensemble music, not only the beginning levels. It is a serious mistake to expect a student to handle an individual part as difficult as the solo repertoire studied in lessons, for the student either quickly becomes frustrated or fails to learn what it really means to play chamber music well. Chamber material selected should be at least two or three levels easier than the students' solo material. Later, once basic ensemble skills are mastered, it is easy and appropriate to advance to more complex literature. At first, a teacher or coach must supervise the young ensemble. Many skills and a modest level of maturity are necessary for a group to rehearse on its own. Part of the instructional method should include how to rehearse, how to make suggestions to colleagues in a supportive and non-threatening manner, and how to make group decisions. A string quartet or other similar ensemble should be a miniature democracy!

Chamber music was originally written to be played with friends in the chamber, or home. One of the wonderful things about chamber repertoire is that at least one composition exists for almost every combination of players. While all are familiar with the great masterpieces written for the string quartet, it would be an unfortunate loss to overlook the many gems composed for other instrument combinations: duos, trios, quintets, and larger combinations, to say nothing of the many works for four instruments apart from the classic string quartet. If students are exposed to the vast body of available literature, they will soon learn that with a bit of sleuthing they can probably find a piece for whatever group of musician friends they might assemble.

As mentioned before, trips of any length serve as great motivators. Such trips can be as simple as a visit to a neighboring town to exchange concerts with another program, or as elaborate as an international tour. There is something about putting a group of like-minded students on a bus and taking them out of their home environment that creates magic. They have a special time together to share their common interest in music. They learn to appreciate each other and develop a wonderful sense of pride in their accomplishments. Many teachers and programs have formed special performing groups with the express goal of traveling to cities, near or far, or to venues as close as the local shopping mall.

While the trip need not be elaborate, it should be carefully planned. Every moment should be accounted for since large blocks of unscheduled time may invite problems. Schedules should be prepared in consultation with the host and distributed to all involved: students, chaperones, hosts or host-families, and parents. Times and locations should be indicated, as well as contact phone numbers in case of an emergency. If overnight accommodations are involved, roommate lists should be prepared in advance; parents at home need to know where their youngsters will be staying and with whom. Again, contact phone numbers are essential. Teachers and others planning the trip must consider the age of the students and agree on safe activities. Policies regarding alcohol and drug use, including tobacco, must be clearly stated in advance of the trip, as well as consequences for infractions. Policies must then be enforced. Although teachers know the students and their families well after many years of working together, a trip is not a time to take anything for granted.

International travel has become increasingly popular for student performing groups. Obviously, such ventures offer a rich experience for those fortunate enough to be able to participate. The wise teacher planning such an elaborate trip is sensitive to whether students can realistically attend. For some families, international travel simply is not a financial possibility. In those cases, scholarships can be worked into the budget, or other special fundraising can be arranged. Some agencies advertise international travel arrangements for performing groups, but these organizations should be thoroughly investigated. Call other groups who have used such services, for some of them may turn out to be mere travel agents with few altruistic interests. On occasion, groups have been stranded when charter flights did not materialize as promised. Travel insurance might be a good idea! The group leader — the teacher or other designated adult — should carry tickets, passports, release forms, insurance proof, and special medical information at all times, just in case the unexpected happens. In advance of international travel, arrange an orientation session for parents and travelers regarding customs, accommodations, and foods and social expectations. Use this opportunity to let everyone know what to expect, and provide parents with schedules and contact phone numbers.

Remember that the Suzuki community is international. Why not develop friendships by attending various international conferences or summer institutes with international participants? An international exchange between Suzuki programs can be special since everyone involved shares a common philosophy and musical background. Heed a word of caution — programs in some popular locations may be inundated with exchange requests, so expand your search to other areas, as well. International exchanges, while exciting for all ages, may provide the greatest opportunity to the mature student since he or she has had more occasion in school to study world languages and cultures.

Many established Suzuki students experience the joy of attending one or more of the many Suzuki institutes held across the country every summer. For some, this attendance is an annual family event. As these students grow older, friendships made over the years are renewed and continue to deepen throughout high school. If the student's experience is limited to a smaller institute that focuses on younger, less-advanced players, the time will come to explore other opportunities. Some of the larger institutes have offerings geared to the older student that will provide plenty of stimulation, motivation, and camaraderie. These may include extensive chamber music opportunities, or a special track for advanced students to work on solo repertoire. Supervised housing provides a safe and age-appropriate environment with unique social activities designed specifically for teens.

Beyond the Suzuki institute lie countless other summer offerings for young musicians. Brochures begin to appear in January, and sometimes sooner; the choices are endless. Some camps emphasize solo work and may require four or five hours of individual practice every day. Other programs stress chamber music or orchestral playing. Sessions vary in length from a few days to eight or nine weeks, and often are geared for a specific age group from elementary school through college. Some situations are highly supervised, while others may be much more relaxed. Students, teachers, and parents are advised to consider various offerings to determine which ones fit the needs of the individual student. If possible, teachers or parents should speak to someone who has recently attended the program being considered. While these experiences will broaden any horizon, the student considering a college music degree derives an additional benefit: summer camps and programs offer an excellent way to meet and work a bit with prospective teachers. Whatever the choice, a summer institute is almost always great fun and provides motivation that can last for many months.

To summarize, imagination, foresight, and sensitivity on the part of the teacher can build upon the motivation initiated in the earliest years of study, and keep older students excited and committed right up to the college experience.

CHAPTER 4
THE SUZUKI STUDENT IN THE SCHOOL ORCHESTRA

The Suzuki-trained student, I strongly feel, belongs in the school orchestra if one exists. Participation can be mutually beneficial. Ensemble playing of any sort can be one of the greatest thrills for a musician. In addition to being enjoyable, it is almost always a learning experience for the young player. Students develop ensemble skills such as listening, rhythm, and rehearsal discipline, alongside the chance to learn a wonderfully rich repertoire. For the school-age musician, however, the social benefits are even more important. Many of these are the same social benefits gained from the familiar group lessons that are such an important part of Suzuki training. In the school orchestra the musical colleagues are often a different group. Instead of the same musicians that the child has grown up with from the cradle, he or she can make music with classmates from school, seeing them in a new situation. Moreover, the Suzuki student is often more musically developed than the school orchestra student and may have the chance to be a leader.

One of the most important clues to a positive school-orchestra experience is good communication between all parties: the child, parent, school-orchestra director, and private teacher. In reality, all four have the same goal in the end: a pleasant, educationally sound experience for the child. Many times this goal is wonderfully fulfilled. The student has an enriching experience making music with friends at school, and the school ensemble gains a fine player.

The Suzuki student should be prepared for the experience in several ways. Often he or she will have heard a concert by a professional orchestra and is excited to learn that there is a school orchestra in which to participate. The imagined, however, will differ from what the child is likely to experience, especially if this is a grade school group! Frequently, the grade school "orchestra" is, in reality, a string class in which the students receive instruction as beginners. This class will usually differ from the Suzuki experience in that all instruction will probably be in a group situation: a heterogeneous string class combining violin, viola, cello, and double bass. The group may look like an orchestra, but the playing level might be closer to "Twinkle, Twinkle Little Star." The wonderful thing about the school music program is that all children usually have the opportunity to participate, including many students for which the necessity of parental participation in a Suzuki program make it an impossibility. Many school music educators are highly skilled and dedicated individuals who achieve miraculous results under less-than-ideal conditions.

If the young student is quite advanced, the experience just described may be disappointing. In other cases, the child is so thrilled to participate that all is fine! This positive attitude may or may not endure. Sometimes the disparity between levels develops into a problem and the student becomes bored. In such a case the student may do better to wait until junior high or high school when some of the school students are more advanced than in previous years. The Suzuki student will be more advanced, as well, but the difference will be less dramatic.

The school orchestra director should understand that, while the Suzuki student may solo at an advanced level, he or she may have little or no ensemble experience and lesser-developed reading skills. This reveals an extremely important point! While the school orchestra will usually provide excellent opportunities to improve reading skills and the motivation to do so, **under no circumstances should a child be placed in the school orchestra if he or she has not learned to read music!** Teaching music-reading skills is the Suzuki teacher's responsibility and obligation. The school educator has plenty of responsibilities instructing the other children. The Suzuki student should not be placed in a situation that is potentially embarrassing or uncomfortable, especially one that can be easily avoided.

The best possible situation is one in which the school director, the Suzuki teacher, and the parent talk before the child becomes involved. In that way, everyone understands each other and a channel is opened for future communication that can help make the experience valuable. Hopefully, each party will come to an understanding and appreciation of the other's point of view, so that the experience can progress with the child's best interest in mind.

Sometimes problems arise. I recall an experience many years ago when one of my advanced young students learned there was an orchestra at his school. He was delighted at the prospect of playing in an orchestra. When the orchestra director, who was not a string player, heard the boy play a fine performance of Bach's "Concerto in A Minor," he decided he would have the youngster help teach the class. This likely would have been a problem under any circumstance, but it was magnified by the fact that the boy was two years younger than any other child in the string class! Fortunately, the boy's wise parents learned of the plan, said, "No," and dropped the idea. The boy waited until later to join the orchestra, and had pleasant and valuable experiences participating in the school program.

An important thing to point out to a student having his or her first ensemble experience is the level of the ensemble music. I have had a student, and more often a parent, complain to me that the school or youth-orchestra music is too easy and not challenging enough for the child. It is true that the page will not usually be as black with notes as the student's solo material. The parent and student should understand that the challenge is not to see who can play the most notes in the least time, but to make an excellent whole. There will be many new skills to develop such as following the conductor, playing in the section, maintaining pitch and rhythm while surrounded by different instruments, and staying focused amid the distraction of less-proficient players. In order to develop these skills, the conductor should select music that directs attention to these matters, in addition to playing the notes.

Another matter that the Suzuki student may encounter for the first time in school orchestra is competition for seats. Many ensemble directors feel that competition is one of the most effective methods of motivation. Therefore, seating within the school orchestra section may be based on a competitive arrangement — the best player is seated in the first chair and the others are seated after him or her in descending order of perceived ability. Seating decisions may be based on an audition for the conductor, a performance for a jury, or a vote of the other students in the section. Sometimes these processes are repeated every term or other interval, and at times students are allowed to challenge a person for his or her seat. Decisions will obviously be rather subjective because a performance is a complex thing and difficult to evaluate objectively. In spite of this tendency toward competition, many drawbacks exist. While it is highly important to have a solid and reliable player as a section leader, it is, on the other hand, unfavorable for ensemble purposes to have all strength in the front and all weaker players congregated in the back. Musically, a mix is better so that stronger players can balance and help the weaker, less-experienced ones. Any experienced orchestral player knows that it is much easier to sit in the front rather than the rear of the section, if only to better hear the instructions from the conductor. Sometimes the justification for competition is, "It's like real life." Of course life is competitive, but I know of no professional orchestra which holds regular challenges to seat its players. Imagine what working in such an environment would be like! Orchestras do hold auditions for Concertmaster or a principle seat, but it is always optional for section players to audition. Moreover, some professional orchestras use a rotation system of seating within their string sections.

In addition to school groups, youth orchestras frequently offer a wonderful opportunity for the Suzuki student. Public school districts or local symphony orchestras may sponsor these ensembles, or they may be independent, non-profit organizations. They usually draw from a greater geographic area than that of the school orchestra, and therefore have a larger pool of students from which to draw. Students and parents usually show a high level of commitment.

There is a good chance the Suzuki-trained musician will find more players of similar age and skill level in the youth orchestra than in his or her own school — no doubt, there will be friends from the Suzuki program! Many youth orchestra associations offer multiple ensembles of various ages and levels. Membership is generally by audition and tuition is usually charged. As previously suggested in regard to school orchestras, the same kind of communication between parents, private teachers, and conductors is necessary to ensure a good experience for the students.

In addition to school and youth orchestras, many cities boast community orchestras, while churches and other organizations may have ongoing groups or special-occasion ensembles. Frequently these groups provide an excellent outlet for the Suzuki student. Parents and teachers should see that the musical level is realistic and the social environment is age-appropriate. Care should be taken when exploring these possibilities. Sometimes when a community learns how well young Suzuki students play, everyone seems to want them. While this may be flattering, it is easy for youngsters to become over-committed. Think carefully before agreeing to all offers and requests, and confer with the teacher! Remember that each commitment requires regular attendance at rehearsals as well as transportation and individual outside preparation.

In conclusion, while school and youth orchestras can be a good experience for the Suzuki-trained student, much care, planning, and attention to reality should be an integral part of every decision to join an ensemble.

CHAPTER 5
COMPETITION AND COMPETITIONS

"Competition" is a bad word among followers of Dr. Suzuki's philosophy, for whom the concept of cooperation has always been preferable. Sometimes, however, this emphasis on cooperation is easier to preach than to practice, for our society has built competition into many aspects of our lives. There is competition in the work place and school, as well as the whole world of sports. Parents of young children have strong feelings about which child talks, walks, or gets a tooth first. Is it any wonder that parents of Suzuki students are competitive over which child moves through the repertoire more quickly or seems to be playing better at a certain level? The Suzuki environment, in which students and parents have much opportunity to see and hear each other, gives ample opportunity for comparison, and competitive feelings can develop easily. Nonetheless, Dr. Suzuki and many of his followers have made a point to substitute a feeling of cooperation for that of competition. Positive reinforcement is the key phrase; students and parents are reminded to acknowledge the accomplishments of others, celebrate these accomplishments, and avoid comparisons. Emphasis is placed on the fact that each student is at an individual stage of development and learns at his or her own rate at a given point in time. Moreover, we must realize that students have different goals. Some will be driven to achieve the highest level of development possible, with eyes on a professional career. Others will play strictly for their own enjoyment. The Suzuki Method, with its prescribed repertoire, can easily feed a competitive nature since a student's place in the curriculum is so visible. What is not always obvious, of course, is the quality of the student's playing or the particular issues he or she might be dealing with. How often have you heard a student ask, "What piece are you on?" All too frequently, the playing level becomes the sole measure of progress in the eyes of other students, parents, and even teachers. Instead, parents and teachers should encourage a non-competitive environment by avoiding comparative remarks such as, "Why don't you sound like Tom?" or "Why aren't you playing that piece?" Substituted for these should be comments such as, "Tom has really worked hard to play that," or, "Susie has greatly improved," to acknowledge a student's accomplishments without belittling anyone else. Great care should be taken, of course, to prevent subtle negative messages that might be relayed despite the words spoken.

As much as he wanted to encourage cooperation over competition, Dr. Suzuki would often say to students in a group lesson, "We will have *concours*"— French for *competition*. He would then have each student play an example, perhaps to demonstrate beautiful tone production. Each student would have the opportunity to hear all the others, and compare his or her own tone quality. The important difference is that Suzuki never declared a winner. He simply allowed each student to draw his or her own conclusion and learn from the experience.

Studio recitals, summer institute recitals, and school and youth orchestras with competitive seating present situations in which competition can be a problem. Frequently, a heart-to-heart talk between parent and student or teacher and student is appropriate. Adults must be careful to remember that music study is all about the musician; parents' and teachers' egos must be kept in check.

Due at least in part to the popularity of the Suzuki Method, there are now large numbers of young performers playing at a high level, technically and musically. The job market for string players looking for performance careers is extremely tight; students pursuing this path will find themselves dealing with competitive situations many times along the way. Sometimes this is a difficult transition for the student raised in a nurturing Suzuki environment. Parents and teachers should offer support and guidance in dealing with the resulting stress.

This brings us to the competition, itself. This may be an event in which students compete through the public schools at the local, regional, or state level or for scholarships offered by a community music group. It could be an opportunity to perform a concerto with the local orchestra. It might also be a large event of state, regional, national, or international importance. Whatever it is, the stakes can be high for the student, parent, or teacher — the pressure is on. Dr. Suzuki often spoke against such events and did not allow his students to participate, saying, "Competitions are for teachers, not for students." Once when Suzuki agreed to serve on the jury of a well-known international competition, he argued that all participants played wonderfully and suggested that the prize money be divided equally among the contestants!

Music, in essence, is an art and cannot be quantified. It is ridiculous to assign a ranking or points to a form of expression that communicates the human spirit. One fine performance may seem to speak to an audience member, while another may resonate more with a different listener. This is true just as one may view a painting and proclaim it beautiful, while another may deem it ugly. Yes, it might be possible to count out-of-tune notes, detect imperfect tone quality, tally unsteady rhythm, and subtract that total from 100, except that performance standards for even young players has risen so high that this "counting" would be rendered absurd! The goal instead is to elevate music to the realm where it is a communication from player to listener; who can place a numerical score on this?

Judgment of a musical performance is a highly subjective matter. Comments from judges are often contradictory. One says the tempo is too slow, and another says it is too fast. One judge may compliment a student on style; another will say it is incorrect. Sometimes a judge is happy only if a performer plays the work just as he or she would! Again, as with a painting, what one person considers beautiful, another will deem unattractive. Furthermore, some situations group unlike instruments together. How is it possible to compare performances on violin, double bass, piano, flute, and tuba? These comparisons are particularly difficult when we are judging young students whose developmental levels can vary greatly with age. While violinists often begin study at the age of three or four, such early study is not physically possible with all other instruments.

Teachers' egos certainly become involved; teachers have built entire careers based upon their students' successes in competitions. However, these successes may reflect a style of teaching based on grooming students for competitions, sometimes at the expense of developing the whole musician. A parallel can be drawn to the classroom teacher who teaches for the test rather than concentrating on the overall education of the child. Similarly, parents' egos can play a large role; it is unfortunate to see children dragged from one teacher to another in pursuit of the one with the most competition winners that year. Finally, and most importantly, are the students. Witnessing a student who begins to equate self-worth with winning a contest is sad, indeed.

Must we then conclude that competitions are of no value and should be shunned? If competitions are approached with the proper attitude and appropriate timing, they can be of great value to some students. In many cases the competition offers a fine pedagogical goal, for contest guidelines usually require the student to prepare two or more pieces of contrasting style or tempi. This requirement may provide the necessary motivation and goal to prepare a performance of a broader repertoire to a high standard. If the student in question is considering college music study or a career in music, the experience of performing under pressure for others is invaluable preparation for the many auditions that will follow.

Teachers, of course, must use wisdom in choosing appropriate opportunities for their students to enter the world of competitions. The first experience should probably be a gentle one in which pressure is minimal and the rewards are apt to be positive. One of the first competitive situations that many students in the United States might experience is the local, district, or state contest sponsored by public schools. Usually the school music teachers encourage their students to participate. The experience is frequently positive, for judges are encouraged to give helpful and positive written comments — many students receive A's, stars, or Superior ratings. In other words, there are many winners. One drawback inherent in these competitions is the reality that one individual is often expected to judge all instrument families, perhaps even piano or voice. Since no one judge can possess equal expertise in all areas, comments should be viewed with this in mind. Offsetting this potential drawback is the obvious social advantage: in many schools the music contest is a major event that not only encourages participation, but also promotes socializing. Beyond the local level, contests such as these often involve traveling to a nearby community by bus, always a significant bonding experience for teenagers.

Following the school contest, the next level of competitive experience may be the scholarship competition sponsored by a local music club. Again, many students have the opportunity to participate and grow by preparing and performing one or more pieces. Written comments are generally provided and may be helpful assuming the judges are experienced with students of these ages and skill levels. Of course, the winners also profit from scholarship money, usually intended for continued music study. All participants should benefit from the preparation, performance experience, and comments. I advise teachers to prepare the student to concentrate, not upon winning, but on the positive value of participating. After all, I usually point out to my own students that winning is only the reaction of the judge to a given performance on a given day. In no way does it mean that one student is the best and all the others are lesser! If a student or parent has trouble dealing with the results of a competition, seriously consider postponing further competition until mental preparation is more realistic.

At a more rigorous level are the competitions sponsored by orchestras in which the winner is given the chance to perform a concerto, or movement from a concerto, with the sponsoring organization. This provides a wonderful opportunity for the winner if he or she is properly prepared for the experience. For further discussion please refer to the following chapter, "A Concerto With Orchestra!"

Regional, national, and international competitions provide the highest level of competitive experience. Involvement in such high-powered competitions must be considered with great care, for they appropriate for only some students. Participants must be thoroughly prepared technically, musically, and psychologically, as well as experienced in competitive situations in general, before entry should be considered.

While competitions may offer financial rewards, opportunities to perform, and moments of glory, one must remember that little correlation has been demonstrated between winning competitions and long-term career success. While success may be had from winning a competition, the benefits are usually temporary: another crop of winners next year will assume the limelight.

CHAPTER 6
A CONCERTO WITH ORCHESTRA!

Sometimes the occasion presents itself for a student to play a concerto or a concerto movement with orchestral accompaniment. This is an exciting opportunity. It might be a performance with the school orchestra, or even with a community or youth orchestra. Even more thrilling would be a concert with a professional orchestra. Sometimes high school orchestras present special concerts in which seniors are invited to play solos. Often a concerto performance is the prize for winning a competition held by a local or regional orchestra. Whatever the circumstance or orchestra, this opportunity may seem like a dream come true. Dream or not, special preparation is required for the concert to be a success and a positive experience for the young soloist.

Being chosen to perform as a soloist with orchestra is indeed an honor that indicates the student has achieved a certain level of excellence. Most advanced students listen over and over to their favorite artists' recorded performances with orchestra, and dream of the day when they, too, can play the solo. What may be unclear to the listener of a live or recorded concerto performance is how much effort goes into making the relationship between soloist, orchestra, and conductor work well. The advanced student is, no doubt, experienced with a piano accompanist who not only provides wonderful musical support, but is also able to accommodate the liberties with tempo, and so on, that the inexperienced soloist may take. Often, the accompanist will even cover for slight inaccuracies or slips that might occur. This accommodation is wonderful, but sometimes violinists and other instrumentalists come to expect it. Even the most skilled 70- to 90-player orchestra with a sensitive conductor is simply unable to make the sort of minute adjustment that a fine collaborative pianist can make. This reality can come as a shock. There may also be questions of balance, as it is easy for a full orchestra to completely overpower a single violin. In a recorded performance, of course, the soloist is always heard because the recording engineer adjusts the audio levels of both the orchestra and the violin. In a live performance, however, the orchestra must play more quietly than when performing a symphony and the soloist will generally need to produce as much sound as possible. Dynamic markings and performance indications in the music take on new meaning with orchestral accompaniment.

The best possible preparation for a performance with orchestra, of course, is to thoroughly know the piece, inside and out. Not only must technical passages be played to perfection and melodic sections rendered with beautiful tone and musical phrasing, but the young soloist must be extremely flexible. Every performer knows the tempo he or she prefers and just what liberties have been planned, but the conductor will also have a concept of the music in mind. These concepts may differ. Hopefully the conductor will be willing to defer to the soloist and follow with the greatest of sensitivity, especially because the soloist is young and relatively inexperienced in working with a conductor and an orchestra. Nonetheless, conductors differ widely in their sensitivity, so it is best to be prepared for the extreme.

Preparation for performance should include a heavy dose of metronome work. The soloist should practice at a wide variety of tempi: the preferred tempo, too fast, and too slow. The object is to be flexible and be able to make music in whatever situation presents itself. Practicing at a variety of speeds should include executing clean bowings, such as spiccato or up-bow staccato, at different tempi, as well. If the musician can only play up-bow staccato at the chosen performance tempo, it could be a disaster if the performance speed varies. As with so many things, preparation is the clue to success.

It is customary in professional situations for the conductor and soloist to meet before the first orchestra rehearsal. At this time the soloist will play through the piece to be performed and discuss his or her approach to the work. The conductor may play piano or may request an accompanist, or the soloist may play alone. A student soloist should feel free to request such a meeting, as it can save a great deal of valuable orchestra rehearsal time. If the soloist and conductor have different interpretations, they should be reconciled in private. I instruct my students to prepare carefully for this meeting by being familiar with rehearsal numbers and letters, and by writing down preferred metronome markings for the various sections of the piece. They should also know and discuss with the conductor any rubati they take in the piece, especially if they deviate from printed instructions in the score. It is important to note that performance editions soloists study can differ from the orchestral score used by a conductor. Editorial suggestions may be indicated in the part with italics or parenthesis. Even the most familiar of traditions should be discussed during the meeting to ensure soloist and conductor are of one mind. For example, I once performed Edouard Lalo's "Symphony Espagnole" with a conductor who wanted to make a large ritardando in the 10th and 11th measures after rehearsal letter D in Movement I, a spot in which the violas have a nice melodic line. I was not prepared to hold onto my D for quite that long! When I spoke to him about this, he responded, "But everyone does it." Privately, I thought of my mother's response to my childhood plea, "But everyone is going!" Fortunately, I thought better of voicing this thought in front of the orchestra. After all, this conductor was a fine violinist! The point is that if conductor and soloist are well prepared for a pre-rehearsal meeting, then full-orchestra rehearsals should go smoothly.

In addition to musical preparation, the teacher should be sure that the young soloist is well-versed in the conventions of stage decorum. A fine performance is wonderful, but the audience is still affected by the visual impression that the performer makes on stage. Performers should look as good as they sound. I rehearse the following points in a lesson and instruct my students to practice them a number of times at home, even if they feel silly doing so. The soloist should walk quickly to his or her place onstage and acknowledge applause from the audience. Without turning away from the audience, he or she should cue the oboist to play the tuning pitch. If possible, tuning should be done in advance backstage so this ritual is only a check-up. After tuning onstage, a nod to the conductor signals that the soloist is ready to begin. At the conclusion of the piece, the soloist should thank the audience with a bow. This should be practiced so it is comfortable — neither too abrupt, nor too prolonged or deep. The soloist should hold the violin and bow in the left hand to prepare for shaking hands with the right, and turn to the conductor, without favoring the audience with a backside view, to acknowledge his or her performance with a handshake. This should be followed by a handshake for the concertmaster and an acknowledgment of the orchestra before leaving the stage. Once offstage, the conductor will usually take the lead, deciding if it is appropriate to return to the stage for more bows, ask the orchestra to stand, and so on. I often suggest that the student set up chairs at home to represent the conductor and the concertmaster, and rehearse this procedure a number of times until it feels comfortable and natural. I also encourage students to smile and look as if music-making is an enjoyable experience! The same is true when acknowledging applause and post-concert greetings. Most performers will feel unhappy about some detail of the performance, but the listeners may not have noticed. Students should always accept compliments graciously and with a smile! Post-concert festivities are not the time for a list of the performer's complaints.

Concert dress is extremely important! Check with the conductor to learn customary dress for the particular type of concert, as well as the time of day. A floor-length gown or full dress tails may be appropriate at one time, and not another. Clothing should be attractive but conservative, as attire should not upstage the musical performance. A classic look is generally preferable to a display of the latest fashion trend. Above all, remember that the clothing must be comfortable for a performance. Students should practice in concert dress at home so there are no surprises to distract the soloist during the performance. A special word about shoes: the soloist will stand and should feel comfortable and secure doing so. Young women should be wary of high-heeled shoes for performing situations. If heels are important, carry them along for the post-concert party, but perform in shoes that are quite secure!

With careful preparation, the solo with orchestra can be an enjoyable and memorable experience!

CHAPTER 7
LESSON STRUCTURE

When I observed Dr. Suzuki in 1973 teaching his own students in Matsumoto, I noted with fascination that his lessons always followed the same pattern. Without fail, each lesson began with tone study, or "tonalization" as we now refer to it. The points for study varied from time to time, as did the musical examples; significantly, these examples were not limited to the Tonalization exercises in "Suzuki Violin School." The important thing was that Dr. Suzuki considered tone study to be vitally important to every student, regardless of his or her playing level. Further, none of his students questioned the importance of sound production. Only after completing the tone work to Suzuki's satisfaction would he say, "And now, something for you." This meant the student would finally play the repertoire prepared for the lesson. The pieces were always played from memory, even if only a part of a movement or work. Suzuki would pick one point to address; that point would always be germane to the student's playing. After explaining the teaching point and making sure the student understood exactly what to do before the next lesson, Dr. Suzuki would end the session. Sometimes if the student was young and other young students were also in the room, they would all be invited to play a favorite piece together. This was done for fun and motivation alone — no teaching points followed. Suzuki's choice to critique only one point made it clear to the student what he considered to be the most important issue at that moment, as well as what the student was to practice, and how, for the next lesson. Dr. Suzuki explained that in this way one point could be well addressed; it would then be possible to move on to something else. The less-desirable alternative is making only minute progress on one or two points, while forgetting several other points that may have been mentioned. Of course, choosing just one point puts a heavy expectation on the teacher, who must wield great intuition in selecting the one thing that is not only the most important, but also the most obtainable by the student at that moment in development.

The structure of the lesson communicates many important messages to the student. Through our actions, not our words, we teachers demonstrate to our students what we consider important and what we consider unimportant. If we ask to hear the same thing every week, even the most stubborn student will realize that we consider this an important issue — eventually he or she will come around and prepare what we ask. If, however, we make assignments and do not ask to hear the material, the student will assume we either do not mean what we say, or we can be manipulated into dropping the point in question, especially if the assignment is unpleasant!

Dr. Suzuki's habit of beginning each lesson with tone study provides us with an excellent model. Music, after all, is all about sound. For the string player, this means tone production. We can work on tone in many ways, using many different exercises. For older and more advanced pupils, scales and arpeggios are excellent. They can be used for a beautiful tone, and they can explore the violin range from the G string to the top of the E string, calling on the student to equalize tone throughout by subtly adjusting bow speed, contact point, and weight. They also require the player to absorb a tonality, adjusting the third — higher for major, lower for minor — and raising the leading tone. An endless variety of bowings and rhythms can also be explored by playing scales and arpeggios; these make for added interest.

In reality, many teachers in the West will not be able to address one single point in a lesson as Dr. Suzuki did. There simply are too many issues for Western students to deal with, as most of them will be required to hone their skills for orchestral and chamber music playing, as well as other musical activities in their communities. Teachers will often find it necessary to focus on additional points. Some will be technical; most students will benefit greatly from an approach that covers many aspects of technique. Students will need to develop their shifting skills, learn to control the speed and width of vibrato, and refine bow strokes. If we make assignments for them to work on these various areas, many of which are long-range developmental issues which are not mastered in a week or two, we must follow through at the lesson. If we do not spend at least a few minutes on each assignment at every lesson, the student may assume that the matter is finished, or that we do not consider it to be important. Hence, a good teacher will plan to at least touch on each point for a couple of minutes per lesson.

Another absolutely vital matter is reading. I have had great success with my students by creating an understanding that some kind of reading material will be covered at each lesson. Excellent reading skills are a requirement for any musician; as responsible teachers we must be sure that every one of our students is constantly improving his or her reading skills. This is not the responsibility of the school or youth orchestra conductor; it is the responsibility of the studio teacher. With this in mind, every lesson I teach to young students includes reading even if there is a concert, audition, or other activity on the horizon. Reading skills are more important in the long run than any single concert. The only exception I make to this rule is when a pianist comes to the lesson.

As I have mentioned elsewhere, I use a great deal of etude material to function as reading exercises. Only after the student develops, usually to the level of the "Etudes" by Kreutzer, do I begin using the etudes in a much more traditional manner. Even though technical matters are being addressed, the etudes are played from the printed page and are usually of such a nature that even the most wonderfully developed Suzuki student will not memorize them.

After these vital tone, reading, and technical segments have been covered, I turn my attention to the assigned repertoire. To some this may treat repertoire as an afterthought, but please remember that if a student's technique and reading skills are in order, he or she will learn the repertoire much more quickly and easily. While this practice may seem a contradiction to Dr. Suzuki's concept of teaching technique through music, rather than through technical exercises and traditional etudes, I see it as an extension and enrichment to be added as the student develops and matures.

Like Dr. Suzuki, I request that the student memorize the repertoire from the beginning. I ask him or her to keep the printed music handy to make notations, of course, but I want to ensure he or she retains the wonderful memorization skills that nearly all Suzuki students develop. The first time or two a student plays a piece in lessons we may work directly from the notes, but I like to draw the line at that point. When the student plays from memory, he or she can concentrate on sound, intonation, rhythm, and musical interpretation just as he did in the earlier stages of study. Memory work should not change just because the level of study is more advanced. If the reason many teachers teach only from the printed page is because that is how they were taught, then this habit should be reconsidered!

After we work on the current piece, and the student understands what I want done and how I want it done, I like to finish the lesson with a bit of review, revision, or refinement of a previously studied piece in the student's repertoire. This keeps alive the concepts of review and repertoire maintenance that are instilled in the earliest years of Suzuki study.

If this kind of regular routine is maintained from week to week, the student knows what to expect, and what is expected of him or her. It also helps me stay organized and cover as much ground as possible. On the other hand, it is also necessary to re-evaluate the student's progress along with my own teaching methods, for it is easy to become personally involved and lose perspective with my own students. In summary, be mindful of the ultimate product you desire for the student, and stick to those goals.

CHAPTER 8
ESTABLISHING A DAILY PRACTICE ROUTINE

How should daily practice be organized? In an "American Suzuki Journal" article, the renowned teacher Dorothy Delay was asked to give her guidelines for organizing five hours of practice. While the thought of spending five hours a day practicing may intimidate many students, Delay presented a wonderful pattern for organizing a daily practice session that fully covers all the necessary areas. Using such a routine is invaluable to developing new skills and maintaining those already in good order. Delay's pattern divides daily work into segments, each one hour long. The first segment covers the basic technique for right and left hands, listing each of the basic skill areas needed. The second segment is scales, the third is etudes, the fourth is current repertoire, and the fifth is for orchestra and chamber music repertoire.

Since most students need guidance planning their practice time, it is wise to consider this basic arrangement as we establish a routine for them. Not all skills listed are appropriate for the young student at first, and the length of time for each skill will vary occasionally. Each teacher should devise his or her own routine for a specific student and revise it periodically. A kind of checklist can be made with new skills added as needed to prepare for a new piece, or as existing skills develop. The time requested for each skill can start small and increase in proportion to the student's commitment and stamina. Multiple copies of the checklist offer the opportunity to present one at each lesson for checking off each skill as it is attended to every day.

In my own teaching experience I have often found that when I first present this routine the student looks at it and finds the idea overwhelming. To avoid this, it might be a good idea to begin with the idea of organizing the session into segments that cover the basic skills. After this has been established the teacher presents the chart representing what the student is already doing. Once the routine has been established for a few weeks the student can usually see marked progress, and tends to appreciate the help in organizing time. I have also found this routine to be helpful to teenagers learning to work alone and establishing independence.

Below is a suggested routine that I have devised based on Delay's concept. Each teacher should create his or her own adaptation. Refer to chapters on the right and left hands, scales, etudes, and so on, for discussions of specific areas.

The section on Tools differs from Delay's model — it includes a few topics that I feel are especially important to young Suzuki students. I begin with tonalization, since this concept is a specific contribution of Dr. Suzuki and something we should not overlook. As I discuss in the chapter on tonalization, it is a concept rather than a set of exercises, and may be covered as a special assignment or incorporated into the other skill areas.

Reading is shown here as part of the etude section, but could certainly be listed as a separate area. Review and preparation exercises for new repertoire are also distinct categories. Please note that it will still be necessary for the teacher to make specific assignments for studying repertoire, reviewing, and preparing new material! Assignments should include what to play, how fast or slow to play it, how many times, and so on.

Early in my teaching career, I sometimes made the mistake of expecting a student to practice the same routine over an extended period of time. Boredom and insurrection can result! Remember to revisit the assignments periodically and bring them up to date; suggest different material to practice various skills, and so on. There should be plenty of room for creativity and variety.

Practice Routine

Assign areas appropriate to the student's age and level.

The Tools We Need:

Tonalization: Tonalization can and should incorporate both right and left-hand issues, but may also include special emphasis on dynamics, tone color, and intonation. Otherwise, these issues can be addressed in the other categories below.

1. Bow arm (the magic triangle)
    Weight
    Speed
    Contact point

2. Left hand
    Resonance (ringing tones)

Technique

Left Hand

1. Articulation   5-8 min.
    Schradieck, trills, etc.

2. Shifting   5-8 min.
    Yost, Sevcik, etc., Kreutzer #11

3. Vibrato   5-8 min.
    Exercises with metronome for speed and width

Right Hand

1. String crossing

2. Legato   5-8 min.
    Slur variations, Kreutzer #2, 3, 8, etc.
    Son File (very slow bow}, Kreutzer #1
    or a review piece or excerpt

3. Martelé   5-8 min.

    Kreutzer #6, 7, any equal-note etude or a review
    piece or excerpt

    Collé

    Any equal-note etude or a review piece or excerpt

Lancé
Any equal-note etude or a review piece or excerpt

Staccato
Kreutzer #4, Dont op.37 #20, etc. or a
review piece or excerpt

4. Detaché   5-8 min.
Slur-separate variations, Kreutzer #2, 3, 8, etc.
(see legato) or a review piece or excerpt

Porté
Any equal-note etude or a review piece or excerpt

5. Bouncing strokes   5-8 min.
Spiccato
Any equal-note etude or a review piece or excerpt

Sautillé
Any equal-note etude or a review piece or
excerpt with repeated notes

Ricochet
Repeated notes, arpeggiando passage,
trill exercise, etc.

Scales

1. Scales (Major and three forms of minor)
Rhythm and bowing variations
(Barber, Flesch, Hrimally, Galamian, etc.)

2. Arpeggios
Rhythm and bowing variations (as above)

3. Double stops
3rds, 4ths, 5ths, 6ths, 8vas, fingered 8vas, 10ths

Etudes

Current material for reading or technical development as
well as review of material relevant to current repertoire.

What We Play:

Solo Repertoire

    1. Current piece
    2. Review
    3. Preparation for new piece

Other

    Orchestra and chamber music repertoire

        May be a larger portion of time if preparing for concert, audition, and so on

N.B. To save time on busy days, basic bow stroke work can be combined with scales. Also, look for ways to combine the other segments by using excerpts from solo, chamber, and orchestral repertoire.

N.B. An hour of practice should always equal 50 minutes with a 10 minute break.

CHAPTER 9
WHERE DOES LISTENING FIT IN?

Dr. Suzuki based a large portion of his method on the concept of listening. Recorded music, as we know, creates a vital part of the student's musical environment. The student is surrounded with recordings of music including, but not limited to, the material he or she will play. In this way every student has a musically enriched environment, not only those born into families of musicians where live music is always present. The constant presence of music for a child is comparable to constant exposure to the mother tongue. When a young child begins to speak, he or she incorporates the subtleties and nuances that are a natural part of the speech that surrounds him or her. Regional differences in speech and dialects are a wonderful example of such learning. Often these differences are too slight to notate, yet every child absorbs them from the linguistic environment. The same should be true of music, Suzuki insisted; all the tiny inflections and shading that the student has heard become a part of his or her musical dialect! To provide an excellent and broad listening background, early in his career Suzuki prepared a special record for parents to play for their infants. This collection included not only examples of violin playing, but also cello, piano, art song, chamber music, and orchestral selections. All were performances by extraordinary artists and reflected Suzuki's admiration for the great performers of the past: Kreisler, Elman, Casals, Cortot, Thibaut, and others. The musical selections were all classic choices such as Mozart, Beethoven, Schubert, and Bach. The idea was to begin at the earliest possible age to develop the child's musical sensitivity by exposing that child to the finest music available.

Some 40 years later, however, the most common perception of listening for the Suzuki student has become listening repetitively to the music currently being studied or music that will be studied soon. Certainly this concept is a vital and integral part of the Suzuki approach. By listening to the recorded example, the child memorizes the piece before ever playing a note of it. Indeed, when this method is properly applied, the results are wonderful. The children learn quickly and with accurate pitch, rhythm, style, and a model of beautiful tone. The student is asked to copy the recording as accurately as possible. The recorded performance becomes a wonderful learning tool.

Several questions arise when we try to apply exactly the same approach to the advanced student. First of all, it becomes increasingly difficult to learn all the notes of a complicated piece of music from listening alone, even when the example is heard over and over again. This applies only to the notes; we have not even addressed the matter of fingerings and bowings. By the time the student is learning the Bach "Double," it is generally agreed that a printed score becomes absolutely necessary.

Another question has to do with the young musician developing a unique musical personality. If we truly believe that the child will make music a "mother tongue" as the result of all the listening from an early age, we trust that the resultant musical sensitivity will manifest itself in new repertoire learned at a later stage. I strongly suggest that teachers make it a point to assign pieces periodically for which recordings are not available. This provides the opportunity to see how the student's musical instincts are developing, as well as the perfect chance to assess the student's growing ability to work from the printed page. The wise teacher will also choose not to play the composition for the student before he or she learns it, as many of our pupils have excellent memories!

A third issue is whether it is advisable for the advanced student to copy another's performance exactly. In the early stages of study such mimicry was an invaluable tool. The young player heard and memorized the notes, rhythms, and style, and reproduced them as well as possible given his or her limitations. Many issues such as rhythm were simply not discussed. The student responded by playing what he or she heard. The melodies, simple enough to be memorized in a holistic manner, were grasped as a whole without the burdens of formal analysis, just as a sentence or a paragraph may be used in speech without grammatical analysis. The learning was instinctive in this process, Suzuki pointed out, just as the child learns the mother tongue. At this point in the young child's growth both the language and the music making represented what the youngster heard in the environment. Original thought was not expected.

As the young person emerges from the aforementioned mimicking stage, he or she is exposed to new ideas and to great musical and written literature. In general experiences of life, thoughts and feelings begin to reflect the individual more and more. This is natural and healthy; we can hope that this growing maturity begins to show equally well in music making! As teachers and parents, is it not our responsibility to nurture this growth? If we always insist that our students try to play every nuance just as they hear on recordings, are we not defeating our purpose? This is not to suggest that listening to recordings is a bad thing. On the contrary, recorded music is a marvelous resource, preserving for us the performances of many artists, showing a rich diversity of interpretations, and documenting performance styles over the years. We have available to us documentation in sound that reaches back to the beginning of the 20th century. Not only can we hear great artists of the past and present, we can sometimes even hear the composer playing or conducting his or her own works. This kind of listening answers many questions that arise about what the composer really had in mind. How fascinating it would be if we had a recording of Bach, Mozart, Beethoven, and Paganini performing their compositions! Since we usually have several performances available of our teaching repertoire, why not encourage advanced students to take the opportunity, not to imitate, but to study as many artistic approaches as possible to a given piece of music? This will reveal many ideas to guide them in reaching their own interpretation.

We should also remember that recordings are frozen performances. Early recordings represent an artist's interpretation on a given day, in an uninterrupted performance. More than one take may have been done, but what the microphone heard on a given take is what you got. Modern techniques, however, now make it possible to edit and splice to such a degree that even a single note can be removed and replaced by a correct or electronically altered note. Pitch and tempo can also be easily altered by technology. The product we purchase in stores has usually been recorded in sections, and in some cases may have been pieced together, measure by measure! Sometimes a specific passage might be performed by a different artist and spliced into the piece. With this in mind we can legitimately question whether the emotional aspect of a performance truly represents the artist. Perhaps more significant is the fact that we are hearing performances that represent a level of perfection humanly impossible in a concert hall situation. If we set this up as an attainable example for our students, we must also educate them about its artificiality.

Certainly listening remains a vital part of the advanced young musician's education, but the emphasis has changed from that of the beginner. We must keep in mind just what a piece of recorded music represents. We should no longer expect our advanced students to imitate what they hear. Rather, we should teach them that a library of recorded music, like a library of books, provides a treasure chest of resources to explore musical ideas, expanding our knowledge of the repertoire, hear various interpretations of artists living and dead, and experience sheer enjoyment.

CHAPTER 10
WHAT IS "TONALIZATION"?

Anyone familiar with the teaching methods of Dr. Suzuki is familiar with the term "Tonalization." The young Suzuki was impressed by the habit of fine singers to precede their practice and performance with "vocalization," a ritual that, according to "Grove's Dictionary of Music and Musicians," involves the singing of text-less vocal exercises that concentrate on the production of beautiful tone and healthy natural use of the human voice. A well-trained singer will not perform operatic or concert repertoire without first vocalizing to be certain his or her voice is working properly. Suzuki felt strongly that this practice should be adopted by performers of all musical instruments. Music is an aural experience; tone production quality is of paramount importance. Suzuki observed early in his career that many students could play advanced repertoire, but usually with an underdeveloped tone. If tone study could become a part of every instrumentalist's lesson and practice session, he reasoned, their sound production would improve. Suzuki took this matter seriously in his teaching and made the study of tone production a part of every lesson for students at all levels. Once implemented, his lessons began with tone study using the point he was currently emphasizing or whatever he thought the particular student needed. In addition to repertoire, Suzuki's teacher-training program in Matsumoto included a special weekly class devoted primarily to tone production.

Suzuki arrived at his concept of the ideal tone by listening to recorded performances of famous artists. Fritz Kreisler was his most revered, although he also admired Mischa Elman, Jacques Thibaut, and the cellist Pablo Casals, among others. Suzuki told of listening to these performances over and over in a darkened room, and then experimenting with his own violin to try to produce the same quality of sound. People who heard live performances by Kreisler confirm that the Viennese artist indeed played close to the bridge with a slow bow speed, just as Suzuki observed from his listening! Suzuki would often joke that he was a student of Kreisler although he had never paid him for a lesson.

In the 1960s, Dr. Suzuki explained this concept of the ideal tone and its production to members of the American String Teachers Association. He asked their help in creating a word that described tone study for instrumentalists. Hence, the term "Tonalization" was born.

"Suzuki Violin School" contains a number of exercises titled "Tonalization." These examples, however, simply represent one idea Suzuki used as a vehicle to develop his teaching points. The printed samples are excellent choices concentrating on octaves and unisons of open strings that allow maximum resonance from the violin. In lessons Suzuki would often ask the student to play a variety of examples culled from his "Violin School," such as "Chorus" from "Judas Maccabaeus," in order to achieve a particular point of tone production. **Teachers should follow Suzuki's example and use a variety of material, not only the printed samples.** Simple repetition of the examples in "Suzuki Violin School," year after year, will not guarantee a better tone. The teacher and student must have a goal in mind and use creativity in working towards it.

A principal goal in Suzuki's teaching was to achieve a free, ringing, or natural tone using the open strings as a model. The first exercise presented to the youngest students is to pluck the open A and E strings, listen to the ringing sound rather than the pizzicato attack, and attempt to produce the same tone with the bow. This is the beginning of a long sensitization process that continues as a part of each lesson. Gradually, other notes are introduced in the exercises, emphasizing G, D, A, and E with the goal of learning to hear the extra resonance possible when stopped notes are perfectly in tune with the open strings. The student actually hears the sympathetic vibrations of the open strings. This vibration in turn becomes a tonal model for which to strive with all stopped notes, even though such an achievement is not strictly attainable.

Perhaps the most familiar of Dr. Suzuki's tonalization exercises have to do with the use of the bow to produce an ever more beautiful sound. When the first few Talent Education tour groups performed in the United States in the 1960s, it was often the remarkable tone production of the young Japanese violinists that caused so much excitement. I first heard one of these groups at Northern Illinois University in the fall of 1966. In an afternoon workshop, Dr. Suzuki explained his ideas about teaching tone production and then asked his young violinists to demonstrate what they had learned. He asked the students to play a wide range of dynamics and tone colors by varying their bow speed, contact points, and arm weight. Next, the ideas were applied to examples from concerti by Mendelssohn and Tchaikovsky. Of course, these are not new concepts; they are well known to all advanced string players. What was new in this workshop was the age of the subjects. These sophisticated variations were being demonstrated by students as young as 9 years old! Most American teachers previously considered these concepts only appropriate for conservatory-level students. Our eyes were opened to the learning potential of young children.

Suzuki and his associates in Japan, many of whom he had trained, advocated that the beginning student play with a tone that was strong, which was considered the basis of a tone that was fine. The child learned to use the natural weight of the arm, rather than pressure on the bow with the index finger. Suzuki emphasized playing with the elbow somewhat lower than many other schools of playing in order to encourage the natural use of weight. In later years, Suzuki exaggerated this concept in order to make a point; he increasingly emphasized producing the largest possible sound by moving the right elbow lower and lower and directing the bow into the string. Greater and greater emphasis was also placed on strength of the right thumb pressing upwards on the bow as an additional way to increase the volume of tone produced.

Suzuki also emphasized playing close to the bridge, with the bow always perpendicular to the string in what he liked to call the "Kreisler Highway," after his revered Fritz Kreisler. As the student advanced and developed, he or she was expected to broaden the sound spectrum by mastering an ever greater range of bow control, achieving not only a full, deep tone but also lighter variations. The assumption was that each student's tonal range would continue to develop throughout the course of violin study.

The three factors mentioned above — bow speed, contact point, and weight — are interrelated and dependant on each other. When one factor is changed the other two will probably also need adjustment. I like to think of these as the "Magic Triangle." A violinist can create an almost endless variety of tone colors by working with these variables. A teacher should encourage the student to examine a wide variety of sounds to make the music more interesting. Often, we become too concerned with the volume of sound produced, and we overlook the different qualities that are possible. Another cause for oversight can be the search for the most comfortable bowing. More control is required to move the bow slowly, but the lovely and soft sound produced may be just what a certain passage needs. The frequent admonition, "Use more bow!" may result in too fast a bow speed for the contact point or weight applied. Bowing extremely close to the bridge can result in a wonderfully focused tone, but if the bow speed is too fast or the weight too great, the tone can be quite ugly!

Obviously the answer to a beautiful palate of sounds is not only to be aware of the mechanics involved but also to learn to listen and be discriminating at all times. The student must have a concept in mind of different tone ideals. To achieve this teachers and parents should guide the young violinist to follow Dr. Suzuki's example of listening to the finest artists, not only by means of recordings, but by live performances whenever possible.

CHAPTER 11
"DO YOU SIGHT-READ THE MORNING PAPER?"

Dr. Suzuki has made constant reference to the language-learning process in describing his Mother Tongue Method. An important aspect of the process is learning to read one's mother tongue. We cannot imagine bypassing this vital part of a child's education. Do we always have the same priority when we think of the child's musical education? Do parents of young students and teachers have the same goals in mind when they talk about developing note-reading skills? Parents of young students, especially those who have little hands-on musical experience, are often impressed by any skills their children develop in note reading. This is understandable since many of them struggle to stay ahead of their children, if not just keep up with them! These parents may have battled with music notation in their own childhoods and feel insecure in this area. Many of them are satisfied when their children can laboriously figure out a new piece of music by counting lines and spaces, and by relying heavily on a recorded version of that work.

Let us make a comparison with our spoken language. What if our children reached their teenage years and were limited in their reading skills to slowly sounding out words, frequently stopping to remember if the letter in question was an "m" or an "n," or an "O" or a "Q," and so on. Reading new material would be slow and difficult at best, and they may be limited to reading stories they had heard many times before. Consider how a child reads the first book brought home from school. The style is often slow and halting and without expression, as fluency has not yet been developed. Expression and emphasis on the proper words will come later. Children's lives would have serious unacceptable limitations if their language-reading skills did not develop beyond this point, yet parents often make the same mistake when dealing with music-reading skills. They remain satisfied when their children have acquired only the most rudimentary note-reading skills. Teachers and professional musicians, on the other hand, envision a goal in which note-reading skills develop to the same high degree as word-reading skills. We hope that our students will acquire music-reading skills enough that they can pick up a piece of unfamiliar music, draw from their own resources, interpret the symbols on the page, and create with their instruments the sounds that the composer intended. After all, this is why in moments of frustration with his college-level orchestra, my Indiana University conductor, Tibor Kozma, was inspired to ask, "Do you sight-read the morning paper?" In the same way we are able to pick up a book or newspaper that we have never seen before and interpret the symbols at sight, music reading should eventually be an effortless endeavor.

Just as reading words enables true liberation of the mind, reading music opens innumerable pathways for the musician. First of all, reading music is the key to exploring the vast treasury of music that has been composed over centuries. Most of us are familiar with only a small portion of the written music in existence. Usually we are familiar with only the most frequently performed works by the most popular composers from a given period. Most popular composers produced far more material than their famous works, and beyond these are the numerous other composers who, for various reasons, are seldom performed or have been almost entirely forgotten. There are many masterpieces that were perhaps performed at one time, but now await our rediscovery. In the last decades we have unearthed wonderful works by women and minority composers who were unjustly neglected. These works can only be brought back to life by musicians with well-developed reading skills, for there are usually no recordings for the performer to hear!

Perhaps more important to our students is the possibility for ensemble playing if reading skills are sufficient. We have the wonderful opportunity to make music with others! This may be a duet, trio, quartet, orchestra, band or chorus, all of which offer the tremendous joy of making music in a social situation. By enabling our students to play music with friends, we are providing one of the most powerful motivational situations available for them. Especially in the teenage years when social contacts are so important, music ensembles can provide a healthy and fulfilling outlet. We often quote Suzuki's goal that we are not using his method to create professional musicians. We can, however, use his method to give our children skills to last a lifetime, as it is almost always possible to find at least one other person or ensemble with whom to make music.

If we return to the mother-tongue analogy, we can analyze the very complicated process of learning to read our spoken language. The process usually begins long before the child enters school, with the letters of the alphabet on the sides of blocks, the magnetic letters on the refrigerator door, and so on. When the child attends preschool or kindergarten, alphabet skills are perfected and simple words are learned. Gradually, more words are introduced and drilled. In elementary school a great deal of time is spent with activities that help cement reading skills. Besides simple word recognition and reading from a book, there are workbook activities, writing exercises, and all manner of games. The idea is to develop skills and fluidity from many directions. The variety of approaches helps to capture the student's attention, reinforce skills, and consider many learning styles. Indeed, reading and related language skills comprise a large portion of the time spent in elementary school.

Music notation is the written language of the musician. If music is an important value in our lives and the lives of our children, is it not reasonable to expect that we will spend the necessary equivalent time to develop the reading skills associated with this language? There are fewer notes in the western scale than there are letters in the western alphabet. We should reasonably expect our children to recognize twelve pitches on the staff. Actually, we need only learn eight as the others are created with the use of accidentals. True, we repeat these pitches in different octaves and, in the case of pianists, violists, and cellists, more than one clef. Also, sound must occur in rhythm, but is this not similar to building speed in reading words?

Indeed, reading music is as complicated a process as reading words. First we must recognize all the symbols. Next we must make a connection between our brain and the parts of our bodies involved in reproducing the appropriate sounds. Our bodies must then make the necessary physical motions on our instruments. Technical skill is necessary in this step; this is the reason Suzuki delays note-reading. The most significant difference between reading words and reading music comes into play at this point. We must reproduce the musical notation in rhythm and tempo. This involves mastering another system of notation — that of rhythm — with another complete set of symbols that must be included with other symbols and integrated into a response. This is also the reason students must be fluent and quick in response to the written symbol.

As we all know, Suzuki teachers delay the introduction of note-reading. This is never to mean that they do not teach students to read music. A well-schooled musician, regardless of his or her ultimate career goals or the method by which he or she has been trained, must possess many skills, one of which is an excellent reading ability. These skills can be learned in many different sequences, but in the end they must all be present. The exact age at which the teacher begins formal note-reading with a child will vary according to the age at which the student began to play, his or her rate of progress, the degree to which the various skills have been internalized, and so on. While reading skills can be learned at different times, most teachers of young children have learned there is a window of opportunity when a student is most interested in learning to read music. Generally this is after the child has begun to read words. Often the child will ask questions about printed music and ask to follow along in the book. Teachers will wait until their student's playing habits are established enough that adding note-reading will not diminish those habits. It is, after all, for the purpose of first establishing excellent posture, rhythm, and aural skills that we delay the introduction of note-reading. The typical Suzuki-trained student has such a well-developed ear that if we fail to take advantage of the child's interest when it peaks, he or she may lose interest in reading and learn to enjoy playing by ear without taking the time to learn notation.

Most teachers introduce some musical pre-reading skills, just as a child develops pre-reading skills from letters on blocks or the alphabet on the refrigerator door. Gradually the process of symbol recognition continues. Just as reading is taught from many angles in school, I propose that note-reading be approached from different angles, as well. Symbol recognition is enhanced with the use of many excellent workbooks on the market, as well as musical games, flash cards, computer programs, and so on. Always consider the age of the student when choosing material! The use of varied approaches accommodates different learning styles and reinforces skills. Games and computer activities make the experience more attractive to the child.

Once the symbols are learned it is necessary to spend time developing fluency in reading notes, just as much time is spent developing fluency in reading words. At this point both the parent and the teacher must show the child by their actions that honing these newly developed skills is a high priority! Regular reading practice is essential. I have found that, without fail, it is necessary to spend part of each lesson reading. I begin with material that is easy for the student and keep his or her eyes moving across the page by setting a metronome at a moderate speed. This situation is structured so the child will succeed and enjoy the activity. Building on this success, I continue to cover a great deal of material and gradually increase the difficulty. I am careful to choose material that the student has never heard and will not memorize quickly; there are many etudes that meet this need quite nicely. I insist on absolute accuracy of pitch and rhythm, but pay little attention to articulations, dynamics, and so on, for these matters can be covered in repertoire study. Again, I make the reading a part of each lesson and demand that the same be done at each practice session at home. Even if there is a recital or other event in the near future, nothing must push reading aside. I repeat this. The teacher and parents must communicate with their actions that reading is a top priority.

Rhythm can be drilled separately, again with the use of a metronome. As separate skills become more solid, melodic material can be chosen that is gradually more complex. The clue is *gradually*; this creates a win-win situation and reinforces student success.

My experience has been that if a student begins with easy

material and experiences success, the reading skills develop to an excellent level. Remember that the goal is complete fluency, just as we would expect with language reading skills. We want to be able to enjoy a new piece of music on first reading just as we would enjoy a new book on first reading.

Once the student has achieved good reading ability, and not before, offer the opportunity to play in an ensemble. If the skills are adequate, this should be a highly enjoyable, and therefore a motivating experience. Parents and teachers should be careful to keep the student from entering school or youth orchestra until reading skills are well on the way. Participation in an ensemble before adequate reading is in order can be a very frustrating and negative experience. The ensemble is not the place to learn to read, but it can be an excellent place to reinforce reading skills. It is the job of the teacher and the parents to teach reading, not the school or youth orchestra conductor!

An excellent reading ability is one of the best things we can give our children. It can be the key to a lifetime of music making.

CHAPTER 12
THE RIGHT HAND

Suzuki said a great deal during his career about the right hand. Throughout his life his principal technical focus continued to be on tone production; the means of producing a beautiful tone are, of course, the bow and the right hand and arm. I will elaborate slightly on the technical aspects of tone production that Dr. Suzuki covered so thoroughly during his lifetime, and make a few suggestions for working on those basic points. I will also discuss some of the strokes that are necessary for advanced playing.

First, before discussing Suzuki's technical points, I would like to address something that has become a problem with many Suzuki-trained students. I have observed that many students, although they may produce a beautifully rich tone, are extremely tense in the right hand. Such tension can inhibit the development of advanced bow strokes. A relaxed and flexible hand is especially necessary for successful execution of the various off-the-string strokes, for which all four fingers as well as the thumb must be able to bend. I often demonstrate this point to students by having them lock their knees and try to jump up and down. Sometimes they can get off the ground, but only with great difficulty. When they relax their joints to jump again, however, flexibility is visible not only in their knees but also in their ankles and their toes. This is the natural way the body is constructed to move. We must allow the body to work in this natural way when we play the violin, as well, for this is how we will obtain the best results. While finger flexibility is frequently addressed, many students experience difficulty. My experience shows that the culprit is often the thumb, for it is extremely difficult to bend the fingers if the thumb is rigid. Often the thumb is stiff because a great deal of pressure is exerted on it. While it is true that pressure on the bow stick can produce a big tone, the resulting loss of flexibility is not necessary because the use of arm weight and a relaxed hand can also create the same big tone. In addition, when the thumb on the bow is tight and stiff, the rest of the arm tends to tighten as well.

The first step in developing right-hand flexibility is to be sure that the student is able to bend the thumb at the first joint. This is difficult for some individuals. If the thumb is inflexible, the student should hold the thumb below the first joint with the thumb and fingers of the left hand and usually find success bending that reluctant joint. After strength and flexibility are developed, it is generally possible to bend the joint without holding the thumb. Many repetitions of thumb-bending will yield the required control.

The next step is to develop the specific motion necessary to use the bow. As I have mentioned before, if the natural motions of the body are mimicked for playing violin, the most relaxed actions will develop. In order to see the natural motion of the arm, allow it to hang beside the body as limply as possible. *[Photo No. 1]* Next, swing the arm up and over the right shoulder, keeping the hand completely relaxed. After doing this a few times, observe the hand in both positions: hanging beside the body, and flopped back over the shoulder. It should be possible to see how the fingers and thumb straighten when the hand is down, and curve when the hand is raised. *[Photo No. 2]* This is the natural motion of the hand, and the motion necessary for the bow hand. Now, hold a pencil in the

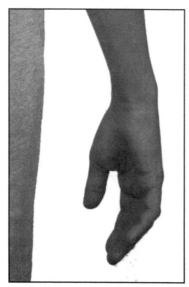

Photo No. 1

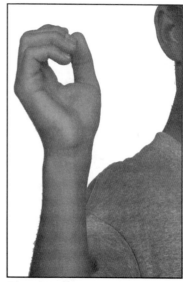

Photo No. 2

same manner as the bow. A small piece of rubber tubing or an appliance labeled as a "Pencil Pillow" that is slipped over the pencil can simulate the thumb grip on the bow and make it easier to hold. With the pencil held vertically, alternately curve and straighten the fingers. *[Photos No. 3 and No. 4]* The pencil should move up and down with the same hand motion as when the actual bow is held. The lighter weight of the pencil should enable one to more easily establish the motion. With many repetitions the motion should become relaxed and fluid. The student can carry a pencil so he or she can practice the motion while riding in the car, waiting for a lesson, or in other situations. When the motion is mastered the actual bow can be substituted for the pencil.

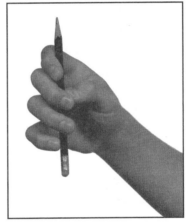

Photo No. 3   *Photo No. 4*

I use Suzuki's "Perpetual Motion" to incorporate this motion into the students' technique. First, I have them play the piece with only up-bows about one and one-half inches from the frog, and at the metronome setting of 42. Each note is prepared in the air with the fingers of the right hand in the straightened position as described. *[Photo No. 5]* The bow is placed on the string; bringing the fingers into the curved position produces a very short note. One metronome click is used for the preparation, the next click for the actual note. *[Photo No. 6]* This process is

Photo No. 5   *Photo No. 6*

repeated for each note in the piece until the piece can be played using the correct motion throughout. I then add the reverse: the piece is played entirely with down-bows, the bow being prepared in the air with the hand in curved position. Straightening the fingers produces the sound. When the down-bow is mastered, the piece can finally be played with alternating bows; each note is still produced with only the motion of the fingers. Playing "Perpetual Motion" in these three ways can be added to the daily practice routine. Gradually, the teacher should be able to observe the fingers moving slightly with each bow change.

The next step is to put this motion to use in bow changes in pieces from the repertoire. Choose a piece from the early repertoire that the student is familiar with such as "Lightly Row." Have the student play it with careful bow divisions using half bows for the quarter notes and full bows for the half notes. Each time the student arrives at the frog have him or her stop and prepare the fingers in the curved or flexed position before starting the next down-bow. As the bow travels to the tip, the fingers should straighten out naturally. Usually, it is not necessary to say anything when an up-bow is started from the tip of the bow. The fingers should already be in the straight position. After this procedure has been repeated many times the motion will start to be natural to the student and incorporated into the bow change. Then, gradually, the stops can be eliminated.

To return to Dr. Suzuki and his favorite points, I was awed when I first heard him demonstrate his ideas in a class with the 1966 Talent Education tour group in Dekalb, IL. I was deeply impressed with his discussion of the finer points of tone production, and even more so when his young students demonstrated what they learned. These violinists played with an amazing variety of tone colors, using highly sophisticated bow control that Americans expect from only conservatory-level students. Suzuki explained his ideas about tonalization and demonstrated contact points, bow speed, and weight. The students then showed how these concepts could be combined, and demonstrated with examples from their repertoire. I simply could not wait to hear the children's concert that evening; it proved to be anything but a disappointment! Their fine bow control was used to provide a beautiful evening of music.

Today, work with advanced Suzuki students from any country should definitely include specific attention to these same important techniques. Our students have the advantage of a large repertoire in their memories that can be called upon to explore various aspects of tone production. A piece from "Suzuki Violin School" Book One or Two, or the slow movement from a Baroque sonata or concerto can be used to explore various bow weights, speeds, contact points, and combinations of these elements. Let us look at these individually.

Bow Weight

Bow weight is a topic that Dr. Suzuki covered well by using the beautiful tone of the immortal Fritz Kreisler as a model. Suzuki advocated a style of tone production that used the natural weight of the arm rather than downward pressure on the bow or a pronated wrist. Index finger pressure was discouraged; a slow bow speed was favored with a contact point quite close to the bridge. The desired result was a tone that was pure and unforced. He used many different exercises and analogies to communicate these points to the student. Sometimes he used exaggeration in order to clarify an idea, as in the case of the exceedingly low right elbow that characterized Suzuki's teaching in his later years. Suzuki wanted the bow motion to be thought of as vertical instead of horizontal, and created many exercises to reinforce the concept of an even tone from frog to tip. He sometimes even reversed the tip and frog or used weights on the tip of the bow, such as coins or metal clips, to equalize the balance of the bow. Of course, the weights also helped to communicate the concept of the bow sinking into the string. For advancing students, it is important for the contemporary teacher to explain that since more weight will produce a deep, full sound, less weight will create other tone colors.

Bow Speed

While Dr. Suzuki often referred to the type of tone Kreisler produced by using a slow bow speed, he also expected students to master the use of a very rapid bow speed. The most notable example was probably his frequent use during the 1960s and '70s of his "Allegro" which he instructed to be played using the entire bow on each quarter note in the first, third, and final lines. Certainly this developed an excellent fast bow! This fast bow was also used in other areas of the repertoire such as the opening eighth notes in Movement III of "Concerto in A Minor" by Vivaldi. The variety of bow speeds had a great deal to do with the high level of flexibility in the bow arms of the students that Suzuki produced in the 1950s and '60s.

Many traditional string players, on the other hand, have avoided developing the skill of using various bow speeds by arranging their bowings so that the speed remains almost constant; if the tempo is slow, they change bow often. This, however, robs them of a wonderful range of tone color and a great deal of potential expression. Louise Behrend of the School for Strings and the Juilliard School has demonstrated a simple and excellent exercise to develop control of a variety of bow speeds. With the metronome set at quarter note equals 60 beats per minute (bpm), the student is to play four quarter notes, two half notes, and one whole note with perfectly even and beautiful sound. When this is mastered, the metronome is moved one notch slower if slow bow speed is the goal, and faster if fast speeds are the goal. After this exercise is mastered, a study such as 'Etude No. 1" in the famous Kreutzer "42 Studies" can be attempted. In my own student days, Josef Gingold had me practice a few lines of this study with the metronome at quarter note equals 40 bpm, and then eighth note equals 40 bpm. Few notes in the repertoire seemed long after that!

Contact Point

Almost everyone is familiar with Dr. Suzuki's frequent references to the "Kreisler highway." It refers to the path that the bow follows on the string, specifically its distance from the bridge. From listening carefully to recordings of Fritz Kreisler, Suzuki observed that Kreisler played close to the bridge, much of the time with a slow bow speed. This observation has also been affirmed by people who witnessed Kreisler's playing first-hand. Certainly this produces a clear tone with excellent projection. Note, however, that if close is good, too close is not better! Some players play so close to the bridge that a ponticello-type tone results. This color should be saved for those occasions specifically noted by the composer. The teacher and student should be aware that other contact points will produce different tone colors as well, and these should be explored for the sake of the music. Any one tone color used to the exclusion of others has the potential to become monotonous.

Bow Divisions

The term "bow divisions" refers to the part of the bow being used: the whole bow, upper half, lower half, and so on. I recall hearing a colleague say a number of years ago, "The Suzuki Method doesn't teach bow divisions." I found this amazing since bow division work is usually considered a vital teaching point for the student from the later part of Book One, if not sooner. Certainly many of the pieces in the Suzuki repertoire present excellent opportunities for studying bow divisions. The general goal is to produce a beautiful sound in any part of the bow. We should be sure that the student continues to develop skills in this important area so that, at any point, he or she is aware exactly which part of the bow should be used. Too often players leave this up to chance and find themselves in a disadvantageous part of the bow; advance planning can avoid such a problem. In addition to the published Suzuki repertoire, scales with variations, etudes, and exercises, such as the Sevcik "School of Bowing Techniques," offer great potential for studying bow divisions.

String Changes

Dr. Suzuki certainly had a great deal to say during his lifetime about changing strings! We are all familiar, no doubt, with the multiple-exposure photos showing the appropriate position of the bow and arm on each of the four strings. Everything emanates from the E string level. When the bow moves from the E string to a lower string, the hand and arm follow the bow only as much as necessary. When the bow moves from a lower string to a higher one, the elbow moves first, and the bow and hand follow. The result of this approach is that the arm remains relaxed so that the concept of using arm weight to produce a deep, rich tone is reinforced. Perhaps, in Suzuki's later years, the low position of the elbow sometimes became exaggerated in order to make a point. In any case, particular attention should be given to the elbow so that it does not remain on the level of the lower string when a change is made to a higher string, for in such a change the elbow has a strong tendency to remain too high.

I would suggest that flexibility in the wrist and fingers be incorporated into string changes to encourage a more relaxed bow arm, and therefore a freer sound. At the tip of the bow, a flexible wrist is most helpful with the hand rising above the arm to go to the lower string. To return to the higher string the hand returns to the level of the upper arm. If the bow remains on the new string the arm will adjust to the appropriate level. To change strings close to the frog, in contrast, the fingers do most of the work. The little finger supports the weight of the bow, curving more to allow the bow to drop to the next lower string and straightening a bit, but never completely, to return to the higher string. Kreutzer "Etude No. 13," played at the extreme tip and then at the extreme frog, is an excellent vehicle for developing this skill. Finally, string changes in the middle of the bow should incorporate balanced movement in all parts of the arm and hand.

Some Basic Bow Strokes

Throughout the years of violin pedagogy, various writers have described so many different bow strokes that names for the stroke nuances can overlap from writer to writer and become quite confusing to a student. If a few basic strokes are first developed and then maintained by the student, the more subtle differences should be easily accomplished later on, when the uniqueness of the music and the performer's interpretation will greatly influence the articulation. All of these bow-stroke nuances relate to the following basic strokes: legato, martelé, and off-the-string. The basic strokes should be practiced regularly and the teacher should constantly check to be sure that the student maintains the skills necessary to execute them properly. They can be incorporated into the lesson and daily practice as tonalization work, while with advanced students, many bowing exercises will lend themselves to use in a group lesson.

I. Legato

The term "legato" can refer to a very smooth bow stroke, or it can also refer to slurs in which two or more notes are played with one bow stroke. For either, good finger flexibility will be of great assistance in making the necessary bow changes. Needless to say, both are necessary and can be practiced as separate entities and in every conceivable combination. Many scale books and the several editions of Kreutzer's "42 Studies" offer variations with combinations of slurs and separate bows that can be used effectively as presented or applied to other musical examples. These examples should be practiced in a variety of tempi. Do not overlook the possibilities of using examples, in true Suzuki style, from the solo and orchestral violin repertoire; the opening of Beethoven's "Spring Sonata" and the "Overture" from Mozart's "The Marriage of Figaro" are two fine examples.

Detaché

This term applies to legato notes played with separate bows, as opposed to notes played as slurs. Remember that, even though it resembles the English word "detached," it does not in any way imply a staccato articulation, but instead means *separated*. With detaché, a smooth and even bow stroke can be practiced with any passage of notes of the same value. String crossings can either be avoided or sought out, depending on the difficulty of exercise desired. The solo Sonatas and Partitas of Bach offer some great examples of material for studying the detaché stroke. Try the "Allemande" from "Partita in D Minor" or the last movement of any of the Sonatas.

At this point, I would like to make special mention of Dr. Suzuki's instruction for the articulation of the two eighth notes in the first of the "Twinkle Variations." Suzuki instructed that these notes were to be played "legato with stop." Instead of legato, especially with beginning students, we usually hear a rather strong bite or Martelé-type accent on both the beginning and the end of these notes. What Suzuki intended was a detaché articulation — not accented but with some space between the notes. This is quite a difficult stroke to master free of accent, but one that will certainly aid the player in developing a higher level of bow control!

Porté

The porté stroke, another kind of legato, is similar to the detaché in that separate bows are used, and there is no bite or pinch involved. The bow dips slightly in and out of the string producing a swell in the sound. Depending on the tempo and nature of the musical example, the swell may be produced with the weight of the entire arm, or with the fingers, alone.

Portato

Still another type of legato is the portato, a series of porté strokes on the same bow which is indicated with a slur and dashes over the individual notes. A slight pause exists between notes, without the bite employed with the martelé or slurred staccato. This was a favorite bowing of Suzuki who often used it as a tonalization exercise. The bow dips deeper into the string with each note and then out again. Suzuki referred to this stroke as the "Casals bowing," and used it with many excerpts from his repertoire. He would often refer to the desired sound by saying, "Sing!" Any exercise selected for practicing the legato or slur can be used for the portato, as well.

II. Martelé

The second kind of basic bow stroke, the martelé stroke, is used frequently as an entity unto itself, but serves as the basis for many of the other important bow strokes. Characteristics of the stroke include a bite or pinch at both the beginning and the end, with a very rapid bow speed in the middle. Preparation is all-important for this stroke. The bow is pressed firmly into the string with the fingers and thumb. As the note begins, the pressure is released and the bow is moved very rapidly. The note stops with pressure, which can also serve as the preparation for the next note. Practice this stroke at first using the entire upper half of the bow. Later the whole bow can be used. While any music with notes of equal duration is appropriate, Kreutzer "Etude No. 6" and "Etude No. 7" are classic in developing this stroke. "Etude No. 7" provides an excellent opportunity to watch for clean string crossings. When going from string to string, most players will notice a tendency to drag the bow in between. If the contact from stopping the bow on the previous note is maintained, the resulting extra noise should be reduced. As for the rapid bow speed in the middle of the stroke, care must be taken to release pressure just enough to avoid a crushed sound, but not enough to produce a "slip tone." All too often, the string is not allowed to ring while playing the martelé. Dr. Suzuki once told me that Karl Klenger, his teacher in Berlin, made him play so many Kreutzer etudes with the martelé stroke that he hated it and did not use it in his teaching. Even if Suzuki did not teach martelé for these personal reasons, many of the accents violinists use are certainly related to it, so it should not be eliminated completely from the Suzuki technique.

Slurred Staccato

The slurred staccato, one of the bowings based on the martelé, will be familiar to the Suzuki-trained student. The concept is first introduced with Bach's "Minuet No. 1" in Book One. This is the first introduction to playing more than one note on a bow. However, more examples occur in the repertoire that are directly identified as the classic staccato: Beethoven's "Minuet in G" and the Becker "Gavotte." In reality, the slurred staccato is nothing more than a series of tiny martelé notes on one bow, usually an up-bow. The same care should be taken practicing this stroke as with the martelé, so that the spaces between the notes are clean. It will also be helpful to be sure from the beginning, when the goal is to play many notes on one bow, that only a small amount of bow is used for each note. The slurred staccato can be practiced in a number of ways. The simplest is to begin by playing two tiny notes on one bow, then three notes, and so on, until many can be played. A specific example from the piece the student is currently studying can be learned with the metronome set at a moderate tempo; after the spot is completely mastered, move the metronome up one speed, then another speed, and continue in the same manner. Another approach is to use an exercise such as Kreutzer "Etude No. 4," set the metronome at quarter note equals 60 bpm, and gradually move it up as the skill is mastered. When the up-bow staccato is under control, reverse the bowings for the down-bow staccato. This is the most reliable way to develop a staccato that will be ready when called for in the repertoire. I would strongly discourage using a stiff arm with an impulse type of motion to play the staccato. While it seems to work well with some players, it does not work at all for others and is often reliable only at one tempo. Instead, with the use of a metronome, any player can achieve an excellent staccato given time and patience.

Lancé

The lancé bowing, again based on martelé, is similar in that the same rapid bow speed is used, but it has no bite or accent at the beginning or the end of the note. This is a great stroke to practice in order to control a variety of bow speeds. Care should be given to see that the bow remains parallel to the bridge. Suzuki-trained students should be familiar with this bowing from "Allegro" in Book One.

III. Off-the-String Bowings

The third basic category of bow stroke is referred to as "off-the-string," or "bouncing" bow. These are common especially in chamber music and orchestral playing, where most of our students will experience them for the first time. It is a good idea for the teacher to anticipate this need and begin to prepare the student before these strokes are requested by the school or youth orchestra conductor. While many teachers introduce these bowings in Book Five with the second half of the Bach "Gavotte" and the "Gigue" by Veracini, other teachers use earlier examples just as successfully. Whenever the strokes are introduced, care should be taken to see that the fingers and thumb of the right hand are flexible. Without flexibility, fine control of the strokes is impossible and the production of a fine tone quality will be compromised. I have found that group lessons for advanced students are an excellent place to introduce and perfect these strokes. Many examples from the Suzuki repertoire can be used that are already in the students' memories, allowing them to concentrate on strokes without thinking about new notes. While this category includes infinite variety in the degree of "bounce," it basically divides them into three types: spiccato, sautillé, and ricochet.

Spiccato

The spiccato stroke involves the bow coming from the air for the beginning of each note, being lifted off the string at the conclusion of the note. The duration of the actual note can vary from a short dry sound to a rather broad "brush stroke." As previously mentioned, the fingers and thumb must be flexible, while some motion will also exist in the forearm and the upper arm. Spiccato is played near the balance point of the bow, which varies with each bow. In some cases, the bow will bounce more easily if the hair is a bit tighter than normal. The player may also experiment with the tilt of the bow. Playing with somewhat flatter hair may prove more successful.

I begin teaching this bowing in Book Five using a broad brush stroke on the open E string with repeated down-bows, making sure that the entire arm is relaxed and swinging from the shoulder joint. The bow comes from the air and makes a small arc. The sound produced should be without accent. When controlled, even notes can be produced easily. I then have the student attempt the same sound using all up-bows. When up bows are well under control, I add alternating down-bows and up-bows. The next step is to change to the A string. When the A string is well rehearsed, I have the student play Variation D of "Twinkle Variations." "Perpetual Motion" and its variation could be the succeeding step, as well as Etude, the Gossec "Gavotte," or any number of excerpted passages from Suzuki material. For example, pieces with varying tempi and those with 6/8 rhythms such as the Veracini "Gigue" or the "German Dance" could be useful. Whatever the material, emphasize even note length and steady rhythm.

Sautillé

The sautillé bowing, sometimes referred to as "uncontrolled spiccato," comprises the second category of off-the-string bow strokes. While no bow stroke is uncontrolled, this stroke differs because the bow is not consciously lifted from the string after each note. Rather, it depends upon the natural ability of the bow to bounce. The tempo is usually faster than that which works successfully for spiccato, and the stroke emanates from the string. Again, the point of the bow at which the stroke is played and the flatness and tension of the bow hair are factors to work with in developing this technique.

To achieve this stroke play a very fast tremolo with the bow pressed firmly into the string at the balance point. Gradually lighten the weight on the bow, maintaining the rapid speed and relaxed arm. The bow should begin to bounce off the string by itself. Some violinists find it helpful to release one or two fingers from the bow. First try removing the little finger from the bow, and then any two fingers in combination. By experimenting with the fingers and the point of the bow being used, the player should achieve a successful sautillé. Again, the Variation D of

"Twinkle Variations," played quickly, is an excellent example to develop this stroke.

Ricochet

Finally we come to the third category of off-the-string strokes, the ricochet. Dropping the bow vertically onto the string, allowing it to bounce and picking it up after the required number of notes, produces the ricochet. The analogy of dropping a rubber ball and catching it again may be helpful to visualize this stroke. Varying the distance from which the bow is dropped, the amount of horizontal versus vertical motion used, and the flatness of the bow hair can control the clarity and tempo of the stroke. Slightly tightening the tension of the bow hair can also be helpful. To practice controlling the stroke, begin by picking the bow up after two notes, then three, then four, and so on. A down-bow is nearly always used for the ricochet bowing, which is often followed by a single up-bow. Think of Rossini's "Overture" to "William Tell."

Students enjoy playing the Gossec "Gavotte" using ricochet bowing for the groups of 16th notes in the last eight bars before the DaCapo. Some adjustments are necessary so the quarter notes before the ricochet 16th notes are played with an up-bow. The 32nd notes in the "Gavotte" from "Mignon" might also be played as ricochet. A resourceful teacher will cull other useful sections from the repertoire.

In conclusion, with regular attention in daily practice, weekly lessons, and groups, a student can develop the basic bow strokes quite reliably, and use them as a basis for whatever bowing nuance a composer requires. The right hand, including how it maneuvers the bow, is extremely important to achieve a beautiful tone and a variety of expressive musical choices.

CHAPTER 13
THE LEFT HAND

The left hand of the violinist has an astonishing job. That job can be broken down into the following basic categories: finger action, shifting, position knowledge and skills, vibrato, and finger angle as a device to vary tone color.

Finger Action

Finger action refers to the finger movement of the left hand and how fingers make contact with the strings. A well-developed left-hand technique assumes accuracy, hand and finger strength, independent finger motion, and speed of movement. Numerous teachers have written material that is useful in developing these skills for the young student. Dr. Suzuki himself provided some wonderful material and exercises to be used as early in a student's development as Book One. "Perpetual Motion," for example, provides a wonderful beginning point, as well as a reference point for nearly every level that follows. From the first time this piece is taught, the teacher and parent should ensure that the fingers come down accurately, cleanly, and with strength. Often we use this exercise to develop strength, asking the student to work towards the goal of hearing the finger strike the fingerboard with a pop. Clearly this "pop" indicates acquired strength, but the pressure must be released again after the finger strikes. If the pressure is not released and the finger continues to press into the fingerboard, a great deal of tension results which could contribute to playing-induced injuries later in life such as tendonitis and carpal tunnel syndrome. To avoid future injury, the teacher and parent should check the fingers from the earliest stages to be sure they are elastic after the initial impact with the string.

In addition to "Perpetual Motion," finger exercises with scale-like passages and others with broken thirds appear in the early Zen-On edition of "Suzuki Violin School," as well as in the recent 1998 revision; these are also useful in developing finger action.

At the advanced level it is necessary to assign the student even more examples to be sure that the fingers are able to move freely and accurately in all conceivable patterns. A number of technique books work towards this goal. The one I prefer is "The School of Violin Technique," Volume One, by Schradieck. This old standby provides many examples that begin simply, but gradually become more and more complex. I often introduce a bit of this material as early as the end of Book Five or the beginning of Book Six, depending on the student's maturity and needs. At that time I tell the student that I expect work on this for at least three minutes per day, but not more than five minutes. This time-frame usually sounds reasonable to the student, so I almost always get a positive response. At first I have the student take only three or four lines, to be played slowly at quarter note equals 40 bpm, one bow per quarter note. I listen for absolute accuracy of intonation, clarity of tone, and articulation. At the same time I look for an exemplary hand position and request that the fingers stay down. Each line or exercise between repeat signs should be repeated four or more times. In this way, the student becomes familiar with the notes as the examples become more complex, and can then concentrate on accuracy. At the early stages of using these exercises, I do not make a practice of increasing the speed of the material for the sake of velocity. While this practice of increasing speed is the traditional use of the Schradieck exercises, and certainly a valuable one, I delay it a bit. When at that later time we revisit the first pages, I then work with a metronome at double and triple the tempo, starting at about 50 bpm for the quarter note, and then moving the tempo up gradually as perfection is acquired.

Trill study is also an excellent way to approach the issue of articulation and left-hand speed. Dr. Suzuki's exercises begin with a one-note trill and gradually add a note at a time; these are excellent, but do not involve the first or fourth fingers for the auxiliary note. Of the variety of other etudes available for this purpose, I prefer to use Kreutzer "42 Studies," No. 15 through 22, which purport to develop and/or strengthen the trill fingers. Use one or more of these studies as needed. The variations in editions such as the one by Galamian, published by International Music Co., are invaluable. Use these variations at a slow tempo, making sure that the fingers strike strongly and cleanly, and are removed in a quick and snappy manner. As Suzuki does in his trill studies, begin with the variations that use only a few notes and gradually increase as the student develops the strength and endurance necessary to play through the etude with more simple variations.

I would like to add a word here about finger independence. As we are all aware, Suzuki advocated developing independent finger action from the very early stages of study, based on the assumption that the alternative "block fingering" tended to make rapid finger motion difficult. My own observation confirms that the student who has habitually played with independent fingers has excellent control of the hand, and therefore finds it easier to keep fingers down when asked than does the student who has kept all fingers down on the fingerboard from the beginning. While finger independence has advantages in developing speed and perhaps also in developing vibrato, there are certainly other situations in which it is to the player's advantage to keep all fingers down. Perhaps the most significant reason for keeping fingers down is that such block fingering helps maintain stability and establish the frame of the hand. In other words, the student should be able to block as well as use independent fingers.

Shifting

Excellent shifting technique is essential for the well-developed string player. Throughout almost 40 years of teaching I have encountered many students who have been taught the first few position-change exercises in "Suzuki Violin School." The remainder, however, often fall by the wayside because the student seems to be doing an adequate job getting from one position to another, especially if those positions happen to be first, third, and fifth. Actually, Suzuki has provided us with an excellent introduction to thorough shifting skills and fingerboard knowledge, but we should follow through. He presents the positions in a progressive and inclusive manner, going from first position through seventh, in numerical order. Second and fourth positions are not left until later, as is often the case with traditional study, so the Suzuki-trained student is just as fluent in these positions as in first, third, and fifth. Certainly, in traditional study when teaching takes place without the aid of the participating parent, it is much easier for the student to move directly from first position to third; the player can find the position easily by him- or herself at the bout, and there is little danger that the thumb will remain behind. However, with the parent or home teacher present, the teacher has the advantage of an additional pair of eyes at home to watch for the proper hand position and shifting motion from the beginning. In other words, there is no need to wait to introduce second and fourth positions, but it is still the responsibility of the teacher to ensure that the parent understands exactly what to look for.

The greatest impediment to excellent shifting technique, I have found, is often a faulty violin hold. If the left hand is expected to hold up the violin it is not free to make smooth, quick, and accurate changes of position. Check first that the chinrest and shoulder pad fit the particular player and make it comfortable to support the violin without excess shoulder, neck, or jaw tension. Proper body alignment and excellent posture should already be understood by this time. When a relaxed and secure violin hold is accomplished, the hand will be free to make easy and accurate shifts.

It is important to establish proper hand position and arm movement next, to enable a quick and accurate left-hand technique. As much as possible, the hand should remain in a position that lies in the same relationship to the neck of the violin, from the first position all the way to the top of the fingerboard. *[Photo No. 7]* In first position, the palm of the hand (base

Photo No. 7

knuckles) should be nearly parallel to the neck of the violin. In this position the fingers will all have easy access to the fingerboard and will be free to move easily. If the neck of the instrument rests on the knuckle at the base of the first finger, all fingers should fall naturally into proper curved position when stopping the string, and even the fourth finger will retain some curve. When the fingers are curved they have maximum strength. The thumb should be allowed to find its natural and relaxed position against the neck without pressing. Note that the exact position of the thumb, both in relationships to the other fingers and in the amount of it that extends above the fingerboard, will vary from player to player depending on the structure of his or her hand. If the thumb is rotated slightly outward so that the fleshy part is not directly facing the neck of the violin, there will be less direct pressure on the neck, and therefore a more relaxed left hand. This is especially true if the thumb has any tendency towards double-jointedness. Such a rotation will also aid vibrato, for in this position it is easier to vibrate freely and to have control over the speed. As the hand moves from first position up the fingerboard, the elbow should move to the right, allowing the hand to retain its position. *[Photo No. 8]* Likewise, as the hand moves to a lower position the elbow must return to the left, to its free position under the body of the violin. *[Photo No. 9]* Practicing shifts of one octave on one

Photo No. 8   *Photo No. 9*

string is an excellent way to exercise this motion. Begin with the first finger and shift to the same note an octave higher with the fourth finger. After repeating this successfully about four times, shift to the third finger, then the second, and finally the first, always at the interval of an octave. Repeat this sequence beginning with the second finger shifting to each finger, then the third, and finally the fourth. Each successive finger will take the player higher on the fingerboard and require that the elbow move farther to the right. If the student begins with the E string and gradually moves to the lower strings, the elbow will again be moving progressively farther. Note that as the hand moves up the fingerboard the thumb will move with the hand, neither preceding it nor following behind. The thumb will move in a diagonal manner from its place on the side of the neck in first position *[Photo No. 10]*, to a spot in the middle of the neck in fourth or fifth position. *[Photo No. 11]* At which position the thumb reaches this spot will vary depending on the size of the hand. To reach even higher on the

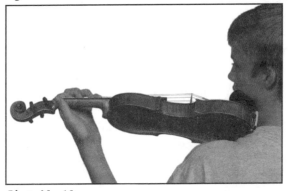

Photo No. 10

Photo No. 11

fingerboard, the thumb will eventually need to leave the neck and assume a place along the rib of the violin. This will facilitate reaching the highest range of the instrument. Generally it is best to maintain contact with the neck as long as possible and resume it as quickly as possible while returning to lower positions.

When this proper hand position and arm movement have been established, the next issue is movement from one pitch to another. In order to move quickly and easily from one note to another it is important that the finger pressure on the fingerboard be released. Various descriptions of this action are useful. The student may think of the finger making an arc or bracket, for example, releasing the pressure on the old note, allowing the string to rise from the fingerboard, gliding to the new note, and depressing the finger enough to stop the new note. This is a good opportunity to check for excess finger pressure. Such excess pressure causes tension in the hand and slows the movement of the fingers. The release of pressure during a shift is also similar to the light finger contact used while playing harmonics. Vartan Manoogian provided excellent exercises that use harmonics in his book, "Foundations of Shifting."

Devoting some practice each day to shifting exercises will go a long way towards improving the student's overall technique. A variety of materials should be chosen following the mastery of the Position Studies in "Suzuki Violin School." Studies such as those of Sevcik or Yost, as well as the previously mentioned volume by Manoogian, are excellent. My personal preference is Yost, which is out of print but might be found at a library. The important point at this stage in the violinist's development is that all intervals and all positions must be covered. In other words, the player must be able to shift easily and accurately from every position to every other. Special caution is advised to be sure that second, fourth, and sixth positions are covered as carefully as the odd-numbered ones, since all will need to be used with equal comfort in order to play the advanced solo, chamber, and orchestral repertoire. Whichever studies are chosen, they must be practiced slowly, carefully, and with many repetitions so that perfect pitch accuracy is attained. Note that often a Suzuki student with a highly developed ear will miss the pitch and be able to make a very quick adjustment to correct it. This may be fine in performance, but if a solid and dependable technique is to be attained, it is imperative that the player learn to hit the mark the first time. Only after accurate technique is established should the young violinist be concerned with increasing the speed of the shifts. Most well-trained Suzuki students have no problem with fast motions!

After total fluency and accuracy have been established, the teacher should see that the student learns various types of shifts and how they are used for expressive purposes. Suzuki and Yost, for example, present shifts using the first finger as a guide note, but for expressive purposes the modern violinist will often shift on the finger of the new note rather than the first, or the finger that has just been played. A well-trained student should be comfortable and accomplished with a variety of shifts.

Position Knowledge and Skills

Once the player is proficient in the skills of getting from one position to another, he or she must be completely comfortable playing in whatever position the hand has arrived. Young violinists are most comfortable playing in first position because this is where they spend the most time! In order to achieve a similar level of comfort and fluency in another position, it is necessary to spend some well-planned time playing in those positions. Suzuki's "Position Etudes" offer "Perpetual Motion" in ascending keys; this helps the student understand the concept of playing the same piece in different positions. My experience, however, indicates that as soon as the Suzuki-trained student understands the hand is simply moved progressively up the fingerboard, only his or her ear remains involved, not his or her intellect. For true fluency, the student simply must know what notes and intervals are being played! I have found the exercises in Volume One of Schradieck's "School of Violin Techniques" to be invaluable in this regard. The first few pages of this book are often used for developing accuracy and speed, but the violinist who works carefully through all exercises up to and including Section XVIII will acquire a great deal of fingerboard knowledge. Each week I assign the student a few lines to be repeated slowly and accurately at least four times in succession every day. In this way, note and fingering recognition have a chance to become comfortable, while accurate intonation can also be a focus. The exercises become progressively more complicated and the notes often seem to be arranged in random order, so most students will not memorize them. Note that since memorization is so easy and natural for Suzuki-trained students, we should see that they are not relying on memory when we want them to develop intellectual skills! As with the early steps in Suzuki instruction, complete mastery is a must before moving to the next assignment if we are to build a solid foundation. Years of observation suggest that all too frequently with Suzuki-trained students, technical material, including the etude, is passed over lightly and not really absorbed, if even used at all. The aforementioned sections of Schradieck, however, present one position and then combine it in the next section with the other positions covered up to that point. This is exactly the sort of step-by-step progression used with the Suzuki student from the beginning: mastering a new step, then reviewing everything mastered thus far. In addition to learning fingerboard geography, a student's reading skill usually greatly improves through these pages!

The ultimate goal in developing fingerboard familiarity, of course, is to best serve the music we are playing. It is the duty of the teacher, as the student becomes more and more proficient, to guide that student in using fingerings that work towards a performance that is musical. Perhaps we should make a certain shift less audible, or add an expressive slide to enhance a phrase. Maybe playing a phrase on the D or G string can provide wonderful tone color. Joseph Szigeti presents an excellent, thought-provoking discussion of these issues in Part III of his book, "Szigeti on the Violin." Moreover, a teacher should consider different options for a hand that is exceptionally large or small, remembering that what works best for the teacher may not work best for a specific student.

Vibrato

Vibrato is the one feature of an individual's playing that is the most unique to that person. Some experts in the past have expressed the opinion that vibrato is so integral to the player's personality that it cannot be changed. While the vibrato is closely linked with the player's energy level and intensity of personality, we must assume that one can learn to control this aspect of technique by varying speed and width.

Past experience with my students taught me to expect that, when they reached the point in their development where a beautiful vibrato was necessary for a lyrical passage, something would often be lacking. I introduced vibrato at the usual time and everything seemed to be developing normally. Sometimes the vibrato deficiency would become evident as early as the slow movements in the Vivaldi concerti in Book Five. Sometimes it became evident with the slow movements of the Handel sonatas. The results were the same: the vibrato was uneven, did not continue through the note, sounded weak, or did not exist with the fourth or first fingers. Sometimes I noticed that the motion actually moved more from side to side and did not produce the expected sound at all. Upon further evaluation, I ascertained that while we initiated vibrato with the usual steps — we established motion, developed speed and incorporated the motion into the music — and the beginning steps had gone as expected, we had not continued the exercises. What was the result? The vibrato did not develop along with the rest of the student's skills.

What is the obvious solution? First of all the teacher should set a high expectation for a vibrato that not only is present but also is even on all four fingers and is flexible and controllable in both speed and width. Exercises must then be assigned and the teacher must check them at each lesson if the student is to realize that they are, in fact, important. This kind of technical work takes time; unfortunately there are no short cuts. It must be understood that a long-term goal is well worth the effort to achieve. I have had much success using exactly the same sort of exercise for the advanced student that was used to develop vibrato from the beginning with that same student. Once the proper motion is achieved, the student begins a controlled oscillation using the metronome. I suggest starting with the most comfortable finger; swing downwards from the upper pitch level and back up in eighth notes, with the metronome set at quarter note equals 50 bpm. After four beats, the rhythm changes to eighth-note triplets, then four sixteenths, and finally six to a beat. When this can be executed with complete evenness and accuracy on all fingers — yes, the fourth finger too — the metronome may be moved up one degree. At this point the student is already able to control the vibrato at four speeds. As the metronome speed increases, control will gradually develop. It is vital to have a well-developed vibrato with each finger, although a violinist will often choose a favorite finger for a long or important note, because situations will arise in which a certain finger cannot be avoided. In some cases in which vibrato has been used for so long that it has become internalized, the student may need to learn to stop the motion before attempting to control the speed. When I give these exercises to a student, I always pick a date approximately 18 months away to re-evaluate the progress. Perhaps improvement will be seen before this time, but I want to make the point strongly that this work is a long-term project!

The same exercise just described can also be employed controlling the vibrato width or amplitude; the exercises can be practiced in various widths. I have found that narrow and wide oscillations will suffice in addition to the student's normal use. While some teachers advocate practicing in a wide variety of widths, I feel that these three will usually make the point. If the exercises are being used to correct an overly wide narrow vibrato, or overly fast or slow, it is obvious that the student should not practice in the width or speed that needs correcting. With speed and width of vibrato under control, endless combinations are possible: a slow and wide vibrato for that warm, rich G string passage, or a fast and narrow vibrato for a special shimmer high on the E string. The goal is to possess a wide palate of sounds in order to serve the music.

Another difficulty that appears all too frequently is the vibrato that begins after the finger has stopped the string and then continues only partway through the note. A true legato generally requires that the vibrato be continuous, through the note, and from note to note. It may be helpful for the student to think of starting the continuous vibrato motion, simply changing the finger while the motion continues. Sometimes I tell my students to start the vibrato "machine" and then keep it going, providing an image that often helps to achieve a vibrato that is continuous. It may also help the student to think of changing the finger on the upward swing of the vibrato in an ascending passage, while changing on the downward swing in a descending passage. In this way the vibrato is likely to continue throughout the tone.

Note that I have not mentioned the issue of hand or wrist vibrato versus arm or finger vibrato. Hopefully students will be able to ultimately use the arm or the hand or, better yet, a combination of arm and wrist motion with flexible first-finger joints. My experience has shown that hand or wrist movement is usually easier to establish in the beginning and is always more relaxed. Some students seem to gravitate towards arm movement from the beginning; when this occurs I do not interfere as long as the motion is relaxed. On the other hand, I caution the use of a vibrato that requires increased pressure on the fingerboard to increase intensity. This usually accompanies an arm vibrato and is almost always a product of arm tension. While this can be an effective device, my observation has been that often this tension is not released; this characteristic is present in many students who develop tendonitis and other playing-related injuries, and is best avoided.

Finger Angle as a Device to Vary Tone Color

Finger angle is another left-hand device that can be useful in varying tone color; it is the trick of making a slight adjustment in the angle of the fingers for certain passages. For clear articulation in a passage, especially while a multiple-note slur is played, we can make a special point of playing on the fingertips. This provides clarity that cannot be produced by the bow in this situation. In contrast, for an especially warm color it can be effective to play more on the pads of the fingers than on the tips. This will also result in slowing the vibrato. Many other degrees of variation are possible in finger angle to produce changes in tone color, particularly when combined with a variety of bow speeds, contact points, and amounts of weight. Experiment!

CHAPTER 14
SCALES

Scales are important! They can be used to cover many elements of Suzuki tonalization exercises that begin every Suzuki lesson: bow speed, weight, contact point, and intonation. Scales carry these basics throughout the range of the violin and through all keys. In addition, most scales involve shifting, one of the most important and often-neglected aspects of violin technique. The creative teacher will use scales to address points, such as various bow strokes and combinations, rhythms, and dynamics, in endless ways custom-tailored to each student.

A former student of Suzuki told me that in his lessons, Suzuki had him play a scale in the key of the piece he was about to play, in order to establish the tonality. He was a strict taskmaster when it came to playing in tune, insisting on what he called "international intonation." This was Suzuki's way of saying that excellent intonation was an assumption for string players everywhere; if a student was lax in this area he or she was sent home to take care of the problem.

Early editions of "Suzuki Violin School" used an A major scale to introduce the fingers of the left hand prior to "Twinkle Variations." Also, current editions include a G major scale prior to "Etude" in Book One, and a G minor scale in Book Three. Many teachers use other scales in the early books to introduce or reinforce the tonality of the piece to be played, and for some teachers these scales and arpeggios can be quite extensive.

I, on the other hand, delay extensive scale study until later in the student's development, with very good results. Depending on the age and advancement level of the pupil, I introduce scales somewhere around Book Five or Book Six. When I do, I capitalize on the student's typically highly developed ear and memory. Rather than taking fingerings from one of the many scale books available, I introduce only two finger patterns: one for G major and one for all other keys. This pattern starts on the G string and, except for G major, always begins with the first finger. Although I sometimes change the pattern so students stay alert, I generally ask them to shift once while on the D string, and once again on both the A and the E strings, using the extension on the latter in the case of G Major. The reason to play higher sooner on the fingerboard is to develop good tone production skills in the high positions. This differs from scale systems that shift on the D string only in keys beginning low on the fingerboard, and also systems that, in some cases, delay all shifting until the E string. Many years ago, when using these common scale systems, I observed that my students often played with a beautiful tone in the low positions but were quite frustrated with their results in high positions. After much thought I realized that they sounded better in low positions because the emphasis on tonalization was in the low positions. This neglected tone production in the high registers. Scale practice that forced them higher up the fingerboard remedied this deficiency.

This is my procedure. Scales are played by rote, since the finger pattern is quickly memorized. Just as with student repertoire, the emphasis is on beautiful tone and excellent intonation. In rote playing, students are not distracted looking at a page full of intimidating sharps, flats, and black notes. Hence, I find that the student concentrates on the sound and usually finds no key more or less difficult than another. The one factor that can cause a different level of comfort is the matter of playing high on the fingerboard. Sometimes a difference in the resonance of the various keys is noticeable; in that case I point out that the more resonant keys such as G, D, and A can be used as examples or goals to be pursued while studying other less-resonant keys.

At first I concentrate on the key of G. When that is under control, in a matter of weeks or even months, I add the key of A and continue to work up the fingerboard adding more keys. The scales are played in quarter notes, with one bow per note, without vibrato, and at a moderate tempo of about quarter note equals 50 bpm. The pattern uses 24 notes, per Galamian, so that when slurs are gradually introduced in 2, 3, 4, 6, 8, 12, 24, and eventually 48 notes, they will all work out evenly. The number of notes increases correspondingly so that the bow speed remains constant. In other words, note values decrease beginning with quarters and progressing to eighth notes, triplet-eighth notes, sixteenth notes, and so on.

Shown below are the finger patterns and the type of notation used to present them. An asterisk (*) indicates a shift. The notes added to create a 24-note pattern are in parenthesis. The top note is played only once.

Basic Three-Octave Scales and Arpeggios

G (Major and Minor)

```
G  (0 2 1) 0 1 2 3 4
D                 1 2 * 1 2 3 4
A                           1 2 * 1 2 3 4
E                                     1 2 3 4 4
                            Play top note once only

E  (4) 4 3 2 1 * 4 3 2 1
A                 4 3 2 1
D                     4 3 2 1
G                         4 3 2 1 0 (2 1 0)
```

All Other Keys

```
G  (1 3 2) 1 2 3 4
D                 1 2 * 1 2 3 4
A                           1 2 * 1 2 3 4
E                                     1 2 * 1 2 3 4
                            Play top note only once

E  (4) 3 2 1 * 3 2 1 * 3 2 1
A                     4 3 2 1
D                         4 3 2 1
G                             4 3 2 1 (3 2 1)
```

Arpeggios

G (Major and Minor)

```
G  0 2
D    0 * 1 3
A        1 * 1 3
E            1 4
```

Play top note only once

```
E  (4) 1
A     3 1 * 1
D        3 1 * 0
G            2 0
```

All Other Keys

```
G  1 3
D    1 * 1 3
A        1 * 1 3
E            1 4
```

Play top note only once

```
E  (4) 1
A     3 1 * 1
D        3 1 * 1
G            3 1
```

N.B. Keep fingers down when changing strings!

When the scales are developing well with various slurs and the student's needs call for it, I often add a drill with various bow strokes such as spiccato. After scales are under way, I add simple arpeggios in the above patterns. Later, I introduce minor scales in harmonic, melodic, and sometimes natural forms using the same finger patterns. At this point I also drill students on verbal explanation of the differences between the various forms, just as I drilled them on key signatures from the beginning of the scale study. "What is the key?" "What is the key signature?" "What is the relative minor or major key?"

To reinforce the formation of a well-shaped left hand and eliminate the extraneous noise of poor right- and left-hand coordination during string crossing, I insist that the last finger before a string crossing be held down until at least one note on the new string is played. In the case of arpeggios, we actually finger double-stops and chords, an important aid in developing a solid and reliable left-hand technique.

At some later date, after a high level of scale fluency has been attained, the teacher may introduce one of the many scale books available such as the Carl Flesch "Scale System," Volume One of Galamian, and Neumann's "Contemporary Violin Technique." The Flesch provides valuable exercises on one string preceding each three-octave scale, as well as an excellent sequence of arpeggios. I like to use the Galamian book for two reasons. First, the rhythm and bowing patterns can be used in seemingly endless combinations to provide variety and mental stimulation. There is no time for going on automatic pilot! Second, the string crossings and position shifts are found in constantly different places.

When single-note scales are well underway, I gradually begin to introduce some simple scales in double-stops. If this is done slowly and at a point when the student is receptive to a new technique, the phobia of double-stops can be avoided, or at least minimized.

Before discussing the left hand aspects of double-stopping, it is wise to mention the highly important role of the bow. So often when a student first encounters double-stops, he or she applies excess pressure or weight with the bow, perhaps from anxiety or the misconception that excess weight is necessary to make two strings respond. In fact, my experience is that often the best sound is obtained when the student thinks of using only half the weight of playing on one note, alone. I cannot help but think of two illustrations Suzuki used with young students. The first is recorded on the Suzuki-Starr videotapes in which Suzuki discusses Bach's D Major "Gavottes" found in Book Three. These are the first examples of double-stops in "Suzuki Violin School." The note C# is played with the words, "one nice note," followed by an open E string and the words "another nice note." Finally, both notes are played together with the instruction, "two nice notes!" Once again the master teacher explains in a few simple words what, to many, could be a complex matter! The other example, used so often by Suzuki, is tuning the violin when a player listens to a carefully-played fifth, and then adjusts one of the strings. Suzuki would then comment that nearly all violinists create a lovely sound while tuning, but that often these are the last lovely tones we hear from this performer! Suzuki frequently used this concept when working with students. At a master class many years ago at the American Suzuki Institute in Stevens Point, for example, one of my own students performed the Bach "Chaconne." Suzuki stopped him after each chord in the opening theme, had him tune his violin and listen to the tone created, and then repeat the chord in the Bach "Chaconne." The result was dramatic. I also saw Suzuki use this same technique frequently with students in Matsumoto.

Another illustration I saw Suzuki use was when he emphasized the importance of balancing the bow equally on both strings involved. He lifted one foot off the floor saying, "twenty-five kilograms;" next he put his foot back down and lifted the other, saying, "twenty-five kilograms." Finally he replaced that foot so both were on the floor and said, "fifty kilograms." The analogy is that each string will receive half of the bow's weight just as each foot supports half of the body's weight.

Back to scales! An excellent preparation for scales in double-stops is work with two-finger scales. This is, after all, what we do with our left hands when we play scales in double-stops. If the teacher anticipates that a particular student may have difficulty with scales in double-stops, two-finger scales may be good preparation. A scale is played in two octaves with only two fingers: 1 2 1 2 1 2 1 2 and so on, and 3 4 3 4 3 4 3 4 and so on. Usually, two notes are played in one position followed by a shift; after the next two notes comes a change of string and a return to the starting position. Have the student practice the following:

Two-Finger Scales

```
G   1 2 * 1 2
D         1 2 * 1 2
A               1 2 * 1 2
E                     1 2 * 1 2 * 1 2 * 1 2 * 1 2
                            Play top note only once
E   (2) 1 * 2 1 * 2 1 * 2 1 * 2 1
A                     2 1 * 2 1
D                           2 1 * 2 1
G                                 2 1 * 2 1
```

And:

```
G   3 4 * 3 4
D         3 4 * 3 4
A               3 4 * 3 4
E                     3 4 * 3 4 * 3 4 * 3 4 * 3 4
                            Play top note only once
E   (4) 3 * 4 3 * 4 3 * 4 3 * 4 3
A                     4 3 * 4 3
D                           4 3 * 4 3
G                                 4 3 * 4 3
```

After this preparation, I usually begin with the C major scale in thirds. I simply have the student play a C on the G string, then an E on the D string, and then the two together using the first and third fingers. After that the student plays D and F, then shifts to third position for the next two double-stops, and so on, through two octaves and back down. If this goes well and the student feels successful and eager for more, I advance to fourths. These are also played in C, but they begin in first position with a single note on C, followed by D and A together, and so on for two octaves.

Fifths come next, followed by sixths, and finally octaves. I do not assign tenths in scales or the student's repertoire, especially if the student is young, until I am confident that the hand is large enough not to be strained or acquire or sustain injury. A violin that is too large for the student could also be hazardous in this regard.

While fourths and fifths are not often covered by traditional methods when scales in double-stops are introduced, I have found them to be extremely beneficial in sensitizing the ear, and very much worth the effort.

Depending on the age, curiosity, and maturity level of the student, the teacher may find it appropriate at this point to introduce the concept of listening for summation tones while playing in double-stops. A summation tone is the third tone, or ghost note, that results when two tones are played together perfectly in tune. The summation tone, or difference tone, may be heard as a humming sound lower than the two notes being played, such as the example shown here:

Intervals

Pitches to listen for

If a student is quite young, it is unnecessary for him or her to identify by name the specific note. However, if he or she is accustomed to listening for sympathetic vibrations, or ring tones, as most Suzuki-trained students are, he or she can generally learn to hear these sounds quite easily and usually will be fascinated by the idea!

Depending on the student, the introduction of the various intervals can occur in one lesson, or more commonly, over a period of time. Generally I do not assign fingered octaves or tenths until the hand is almost fully grown. I realize that some teachers feel that these intervals will help stretch the hand, but my experience has shown that injury is possible to the developing hand and I would prefer to take no chances. If the student's repertoire requires an occasional tenth, remember that there is less stress to the hand if the upper note is placed first and the first finger reaches back for the lower note.

I have found it helpful to many students to remember that the bass note of the double-stop occurs on the bottom with thirds, on the top with fourths, on the bottom with fifths, and on the top again with sixths, alternating with each scale.

As the student becomes comfortable, accurate, and proficient with the double-stop scales, the tempo may be increased from the **very slow** starting point of half note equals 40 bpm or so, while slurs, various rhythms, and bowings may also be introduced.

To be sure the student actually practices all arpeggios and double-stops that have been assigned, I give my students a checklist to use for home practice. I may ask them to show this to me at any given time! I am careful to explain to them which items they should do each week. Of course, variations on this checklist can be made according to age, advancement level, and other concerns. It is also important to remember that if the student is expected to follow through with scales, or anything else, for that matter, the teacher must actually listen to the material at the lesson. This may be difficult when there are so many important things to deal with at each lesson, but what a teacher covers in a lesson gives a strong message to the student about what is considered important. I often deal with the scale issue by having a "scale of the week." I ask for a different scale each week, unless the student has not yet progressed that far, and keep track of my requests.

CHAPTER 15
ETUDES AND SUCH

The Suzuki Method, aside from Suzuki's short piece in Book One of "Suzuki Violin School," has become known as an approach that eschews the etudes and scales traditionally associated with serious violin study. Of course, this "serious violin study" refers to the many volumes of material that have been composed over centuries for pedagogical purposes. These are a large body of study material at all levels that deal with every aspect of technique — etudes. Much of this material is excellent, since the art of teaching the violin has become highly sophisticated during the past three centuries.

Suzuki preferred to develop the young player by using a carefully thought-out, select repertoire of solo material. His curriculum was meticulously chosen and arranged so that if the teacher was trained in the proper application of the method, the student would develop to a high level without the etudes and scales thought by many to be dull and boring. Indeed, this was accomplished many times. Dr. Suzuki and numerous associates in Japan, as well as many teachers in the rest of the world, produced excellent violinists using only the ten volumes of "Suzuki Violin School," followed by standard solo repertoire as the student matured. In my early teaching years I did the same. The first students I took through the curriculum performed major concert pieces — concerti of Mendelssohn, Wieniawski, Vieuxtemps, Barber, Khachaturian, and Paganini; the Saint-Saëns "Introduction and Rondo Capricioso"; the Bach "Chaconne" — including a number of solos with professional orchestras such as the Minnesota Orchestra, before doing any traditional scale or etude study. When I told this to non-Suzuki colleagues in the 1970s, they did not believe me. In reality, although I did not use etudes, I had given much careful attention to the technical development of these students. I had done this in the Suzuki style by choosing music to deal with specific technical issues and then by watching vigilantly over my students to be sure they practiced passages carefully.

I often custom-made special exercises, i.e., etudes, to prepare for anticipated difficulties or solve problems.

In retrospect I have found, as have many other successful Suzuki teachers, that the ideas and materials of outstanding, non-Suzuki, pedagogical minds can be put to good use with our students to give them an even better foundation. This is not because my goal is to prepare every student for a career as a professional musician. This has never been my goal, as it is never the goal of any true follower of the Suzuki philosophy. My goal is to guide the student to develop his or her potential to the highest possible level. If the student decides at a later date that a career in music is his or her goal, then I certainly want to have given that student the kind of foundation that would make attaining that goal a possibility.

Etudes are compositions that have been written for the specific purpose of developing technique, and often focus on a single point like fast fingers, double stops, or a particular bow stroke. Often this point is practiced in many keys and appears in various permutations. A few of these pieces, such as the Paganini "Caprices," were intended for performance. Most of them, however, were intended to be used by the musician, often a student, to advance his or her technical capacity. There is a wealth of etude material for the violin that offers great potential for growth. It is comprehensive and often graded according to difficulty. This is the way most violinists of the past developed their playing skills. Much of this material, as valuable as it is, has little musical interest. For this reason students frequently shun practicing their etudes! But my experience with many Suzuki-trained students suggests that etudes introduced at the right time and in the correct manner, can actually be something new and interesting in contrast to the student's previous steady diet of solo repertoire. In addition, the young violinist can rely on a much broader foundation so that learning new repertoire is easier in the future. Reading skills can be greatly enhanced, moreover, and this is a plus for any musician, not only the Suzuki-trained student.

I introduce etudes gradually to my students. The introduction seems gradual, at least, when compared to the traditional usage. After many years of experimenting I have developed an approach that has proven to be very successful. Here it is.

After the students learn the basics of note reading — i.e., recognition of the symbols involved and their relationship to the sounds being reproduced — I find that they all need a great deal of drill and reinforcement in order to become truly fluent readers. The vast supply of graded etudes provides a good resource. The students should be challenged gently with unfamiliar music that deviates from the expected musical paths of the Baroque and Classical forms with which they are extremely familiar. Their ears are so well trained and their memories so fine that often they do not really read the notes of the solos in front of them. In addition, most of these etudes have many key changes and accidentals that provide further benefit for reading practice. Another argument for reading practice is that students will rarely memorize pieces after only a few playings. (This feat, however, is not at all uncommon with Suzuki-trained students!)

I begin with the "First Etudes for Strings," compiled by Whistler and Hummel and published by Rubank Publications. The examples used are short, simple, and arranged as four selections on facing pages that are in the same key and that usually incorporate similar rhythmic patterns and/or bowing techniques. The students are instructed to play with a metronome set at a comfortable tempo. The purpose of this, other than to ensure a steady tempo, is to keep the eyes moving across the page and the mind thinking ahead, promoting fluency and preventing the eyes from stopping at each note. This is similar to the type of drill that is used in elementary school to promote quicker reading of words. I keep the students on a page or two until their performance is accurate and fluent without stops or hesitation, before moving along to new examples. At first progress is slow, but it soon quickens as the student gains confidence and learns that he or she can enjoy sight-reading and can succeed at it.

As reading skills develop, I gradually introduce examples that are increasingly more difficult, longer, and incorporate positions other than first position. I feel it is essential that the students cover a large quantity of material that incorporates many tonalities and rhythmic patterns. I never use all the examples in a given volume and generally avoid the ones obviously intended for finger strengthening, and so on. I tailor the number and choice of selection to the individual student, always use the metronome, and demand an increasingly high level of accuracy.

It is quite some time before I begin to use the etudes in the manner that we traditionally think of them: working on various bow strokes, bow divisions, velocity, and so on. At first I am interested only in cementing excellent reading skills. The other technical and musical skills should already be developing through the solo repertoire just as they have been doing up until this time in the student's Suzuki study. Since students begin with selections that are easily mastered, they do not usually come to dread anything with the word "Etude" printed on the cover of the book. At some point, usually while assigning Jakob Dont's "24 Studies," Opus 37, I gradually begin to work in some of the more traditional studies of bow strokes and the like. By the time the student reaches Kreutzer's "42 Studies" I am making increasing use of bowing and rhythmic variations, as I feel that this is the best way to give a young developing violinist a thorough foundation. In this respect, we as Suzuki teachers must not ignore the valuable contributions of several centuries of outstanding pedagogical thought. Dr. Suzuki's findings should be viewed as an enormous contribution, one of the greatest in history, in fact, but not a complete replacement.

Here is the sequence of reading and etude material that I generally follow:

READING/ETUDE SEQUENCE

1. Whistler and Hummel, "First Etude Album for Violin," Rubank Publications

2. Levenson, "Fifty Selected Studies in First Position," Theodore Presser Company

3. Wohlfahrt, "Foundation Studies for the Violin," Vol. 2, Carl Fischer

4. Kayser, "36 Etudes," Kalmus

5. Dont, "24 Studies," Opus 37, Galamian, International Music Company

6. Kreutzer, "42 Studies," Galamian, International Music Company

7. Rode, "24 Caprices," Galamian Edition, International Music Company

8. Gavinies, "24 Studies," Galamian Edition, International Music Company

9. Dont, "Etudes and Caprices," Opus 35, Galamian Edition, International Music Company

10. Paganini, "24 Caprices," Opus 1, various editions

Please remember that the sequence cannot be the same for every student. I use more for some and less for others. I never use everything in a particular volume, and often only a portion of the book, as in the case of the Kayser etudes where I generally use only the last part. The first part is exclusively first position which has generally been covered sufficiently in the previous volumes of studies. It is important that the teacher be careful to present a logical progression of material and not make large leaps in difficulty between collections. The security that the student develops from being able to master what is presented, is as important at this point as it was when that same student was younger and in an earlier stage of development. I have often seen students who had been given Kreutzer, or even Paganini "Caprices," much too early. In these cases the teacher was probably encouraged by the fact that the student had done such a good job of preparing the previous works assigned. The importance of filling in all the gaps with studies such as Wohlfahrt and Dont, Opus 37, in order to build a foundation that is reliable, cannot be underestimated.

Now for a few notes about the etudes selected and the editions used. From the Dont, Opus 37, onward, with the possible exception of the Paganini "Caprices" which not every student will reach, I am partial to the editions by Ivan Galamian. They are among the only versions of the classic etudes that have been revised in nearly a century, and they present marvelous pedagogical thought, especially in the matter of fingering. My experience has been that they help the student to acquire a truly comprehensive knowledge of the fingerboard, and do not ignore such vital matters as second and fourth positions. They introduce many extended and contracted enharmonic fingerings, as well. Suzuki would, no doubt, approve!

CHAPTER 16
WHAT ABOUT
THE MOZART CONCERTI?

Two Mozart concerti constitute Books Nine and Ten of "Suzuki Violin School," but many teachers question the advisability of teaching these immediately following Book Eight. There are a number of reasons for this. While a few students will be well prepared and eager to play these important and lovely concerti, most students will be better served by delaying this study into the future. A number of factors should be considered when making this significant decision about repertoire.

First of all, a successful performance of Mozart requires a level of control, both left-hand and right-hand, as well as musical expression considerably beyond that which is necessary for the repertoire in the previous eight volumes of "Suzuki Violin School." Intonation must be impeccable in order to present the music with the purity that the style requires. Shifting must be clean and free from excessive slides, and the vibrato must be controllable in a variety of speeds and widths. The bow arm must be developed enough to be able to handle a wide range of strokes, including off-the-string bowings and a perfect legato, in order to execute the many subtle nuances that are characteristic and expected in a performance of Mozart. Many Suzuki-trained students simply do not have all of these techniques comfortably under control at this point in their development. Certainly it is possible to develop the necessary skills while studying the concerti, but my experience has been that many students find this approach frustrating: it simply takes too long to bring the required skills to the desired level for a fine performance.

A second consideration has to do with pacing of the student's study. Through Book Seven, Suzuki used a pattern that alternates pieces requiring extended preparation time with less demanding pieces that are quickly learned and reward the student for past hard work. By Book Eight, as a result, a certain momentum has usually established itself as these pieces are learned. Even the more complicated movements of the Veracini "Sonata" do not take an excessive length of time for most students to learn. The result is a level of satisfaction and feeling of accomplishment in the individual student's ability to learn new material. When we follow this directly with a difficult movement of a Mozart concerto including a Joachim cadenza, frustration is commonly the result. Mozart simply takes much longer to learn and to achieve success. If the technique can be more highly developed before the Mozart is attempted, the material is more quickly learned and a great deal of frustration avoided.

A third and very important factor has to do with the musical maturity of many young students. The Baroque pieces that make up by far the largest body of the repertoire in the preceding eight volumes are rhythmically and harmonically very clear. Phrasing is predictable and form is simple and straightforward. The emotional content of these pieces is easy to grasp, as well. Suzuki understood that such music appeals readily to youngsters and is quickly accessible to them. Mozart, however, is considerably more complex and sophisticated. While a very few young students might relate to the subtle nuances and ultra-refined emotional expression, many simply are not at the appropriate level of maturity to relate to these works. This is a developmental issue. In time, most young musicians will relish what Mozart has to say and be eager to study and perform these wonderful concerti. Until students are so motivated, there is a great body of other repertoire that can help a young violinist acquire much of the technique called for in Mozart. Time and greater exposure to a wide range of music will help form musical taste and a desire to play a Mozart concerto. In fact, I have found a great deal of success in simply waiting for the student to request Mozart. This level of interest is in itself a great indicator of a heightened level of musical understanding.

On the other hand, when students have studied Mozart at a very early stage and found the challenge to be too much, they are sometimes not eager to play these works later on when they are more prepared to do them justice. They either have unpleasant memories of the earlier experience, or think of these works as "Suzuki pieces": student pieces, and not part of the standard concert repertoire. This is indeed unfortunate, a situation that we as teachers must try to avoid.

What about the student, who, the teacher is convinced, is technically ready and who has also expressed eagerness to begin the Mozart "Concerto in A Major" or "Concerto in D Major" immediately after Book Eight? I would suggest that a few matters be given serious thought before moving on. The first has to do with which edition to use. The editions of "Suzuki Violin School" are taken almost literally from those published by Joseph Joachim a century ago. It was logical for Suzuki to make this choice for several reasons. First of all, Joachim had been a major force in bringing works from the classical period back into the repertoire and was famous for his interpretations of them. Secondly, Karl Klengler, Suzuki's teacher in Berlin, had been a pupil of Joachim and certainly would have carried on the traditions of his master. As was the custom at that time, Joachim took liberties editing Mozart's original manuscript. Many articulations or bowings, some dynamics, and even notes have been changed in a few cases, especially in the "Concerto in A Major." Further, there are many differences in both concerti in the realization of appoggiaturas — whether they should be played short or long. Perhaps these changes were made to express the artistic taste of the editor. Perhaps Joachim thought he was correcting errors. We cannot be sure. Joachim's cadenzas, published in Book Nine and Ten of "Suzuki Violin School," are highly inventive, virtuosic, and lovely, and have been so widely performed that many violinists cannot imagine using anything else; they seem to be part of the concerti, we have heard them played that way so many times.

Instead of using Joachim's editions full of liberties, teachers may wish to seriously consider using an urtext edition. An urtext edition prints the music exactly as it is found in the original sources. If an original manuscript is available, as it is in the case of the two works being discussed, that will be the source. If there is more than one manuscript in the composer's own hand, differences will be cited. If no original manuscript in the composer's hand is available, first editions may be used in an attempt to present the material as closely as possible to the way in which the composer wrote it. Any deviations from the original or corrections of apparent errors or inconsistencies are noted as such by the editor. The same is true of editorial suggestions such as fingerings or bowing changes; these are always indicated by italics, different type, or other similar means to indicate an editorial mark. This gives the performer the opportunity to make his or her own decisions based on the composer's intentions. Current trends in performance practices and scholarly research require that performers adhere more closely to the composer's original intentions than to the whims of the performer. We do know, after all, that Mozart was a fine violinist and wrote these pieces for his own performances. Despite differences between his bow and our modern ones, and alterations to the instrument since his time, Mozart clearly knew how various bowings would sound and what would be playable. Some of Mozart's own bowings, such as the final passage before the cadenza in Movement I of "Concerto in A Major," are actually easier to execute than Joachim's!

Regardless of how authentic one is with bowings, the matter of fingerings is quite different, for a great deal of thought has been given to fingerings since Joachim did his editing a century ago. We no longer have the same concept of a tasteful and expressive shift, for example. We know from the earliest recorded examples, one of which was actually made by Joseph Joachim, that large audible slides were very much in vogue in the late 19th century. Current performance practice, on the other hand, would suggest using higher positions than Mozart would have used, and at the same time, substantially minimizing most audible shifts. Many shifts are currently made where half steps occur in the melodic line, also to avoid hearing the change of position. In addition, current practice relies much more heavily on second, fourth, and sixth positions. This results in passage work that is much cleaner and again, free from all but a few audible shifts.

Many teachers and students will choose to consult with several of the excellent performance editions available, in order to compare ideas from various editors. These editions may or may not adhere to the original, but have been published for the express purpose of providing bowing and fingering suggestions that the editor feels will be practical and/or have artistic merit. By researching a variety of editions, the player can come up with solutions that work from the technical and musical points of view.

Regarding the cadenzas, those by Joachim represent violin technique and harmonies as they existed in the late 19th century. In Mozart's time, however, it was customary for the player to improvise a cadenza, perhaps even spontaneously during the performance. This art of improvisation was part of every musician's training. Since this is not a common part of most current musicians' training, we rely on the various published cadenzas unless we choose to write our own! While we do not have examples of Mozart's own cadenzas for his violin concerti, we do have examples of those he wrote for some of his piano concerti as well as for the "Symphonie Concertante in E flat" K.364 and the "Concertone in C Major", K.190. From these we can deduce a great deal about what was customary for a cadenza in the late 18th century. The 18th century cadenza uses material from the movement, rarely goes beyond the key of the movement, and does not exceed the technical difficulty of the composition. These are significant differences from the cadenzas by Joachim. Now we have cadenzas that have been written and published in recent times to adhere to the performance practices of Mozart's time. Of particular note are those by Franz Beyer. They are highly effective, and since they do not exceed the technical difficulties of the concerto, they do not bog down the student at this point of study. Another interesting option is the material written by Robert Levin. He presents a section of a cadenza and follows it with two or more optional sections. After the section the performer chooses, Levin provides more options. This presentation gives the player an opportunity to express individual choice and to gain something of a feeling for what it might be like to improvise one's own cadenza. The pianist Paul Badura-Skoda has also published cadenzas for some of the violin concerti in a style closer to that of the 18th century.

Other cadenzas are also available, either in a style of the 18th century or in more virtuosic styles by famous performers such as Kreisler and Heifetz.

Preparation and performance of Mozart's lovely violin concerti can be a life-long project. They contain such beauty and so many artistic choices that we can spend years studying them and always feel that there is room for improvement and change. This is precisely why we should carefully consider at which point in a student's training we introduce these works. May it be a rewarding experience for whoever takes on the challenge.

CHAPTER 17
WHERE DO WE GO
AFTER BOOK EIGHT?

When students begin the journey through the curriculum of "Suzuki Violin School," they all start from basically the same point. That is, they all have everything to learn about playing the violin. The many skills and the large body of knowledge related to playing are all down the road ahead of them. In the greater sense it is not necessary for the teacher to make difficult decisions about what to do next, as all the basic skills must be acquired; the skills may be added in a variety of sequences but they are all necessary and must be learned. Of course, Suzuki provided us with a marvelous learning sequence in "Suzuki Violin School" that is both comprehensive and highly workable. Individual teachers may make slight variations in presentation, but for the most part we learned that Suzuki's many years of research and experience creating his curriculum resulted in a learning sequence we can follow with highly predictable results.

More difficult decisions face the teacher after the student has completed the Suzuki curriculum. My own experience indicates that when students complete Book Eight or Book Ten, depending on which choice was made about the Mozart concerti, they exhibit many levels of development both musically and technically, and may have many different personal goals. Each individual student will by this time demonstrate unique strengths and weaknesses as well as likes and dislikes of musical styles. The teacher has the responsibility to build on individual strengths and to try to strengthen the areas that are weak. If, for example, the student shows a strong affinity for music of the Baroque, which many Suzuki-trained violinists do, the teacher's responsibility is to introduce repertoire of other periods and styles in order to expand the horizons and capabilities of that young musician. Sometimes a young violinist wants to play nothing but virtuoso pieces by late 19th-century composers, and plays them with great facility and style. It would be a mistake to continue giving this student only pieces of this genre and neglect building a repertoire that also includes the classical and contemporary periods as well as sonatas with piano.

Another important consideration is the fact that not all students have the same goals. Some students will make it obvious that the violin is an important part of life, clearly a high priority, and perhaps a future career choice. I have always tried to give each of my students the kind of foundation that would make possible a professional career in music should he or she choose this path. I would hate to think that, even if such a decision were made at a relatively later date, they might be kept from success because of inadequate early instruction. Naturally, not all of our students decide on a career with the violin. Such a career was never Suzuki's goal from the beginning. When a student who has excelled and could easily choose to pursue the profession decides instead to go another direction, the parent and teacher who have put so much time and effort into the musical upbringing must remember the original goals and not express disappointment. Hopefully we have given each student a solid foundation as well as a love of music and the violin. Many of our students will fall into the "happy amateur" category in their adult lives, thereby achieving our original goals. These students may not be interested in being challenged to develop technique to the highest possible level, striving to play the Tchaikovsky "Concerto" or Paganini "Caprices," for example. They may be much more interested in playing some shorter pieces or sonatas with a pianist from their circle of family and friends. Such interests and desires must be accommodated so that music can continue to be an important and vital part of these students' lives. Of course, such priorities can quickly change with young people; if we have been careful to focus our attention on good playing habits as well as repertoire, we should be able to make a slight shift of direction right along with the student.

If students are not expected to follow a specific curriculum, it is much easier to accommodate the individual's needs and/or goals. Until Book Eight or Book Ten, Suzuki students followed a set order of repertoire which, while highly motivating to some, might have been demoralizing at times to others. If students are finally given their own individual repertoire at this point in their study, they often feel relief from the pressure to move through the set curriculum at the same rate as their colleagues or to be judged by their position in the books. I have often seen a student develop a unique sense of identity with the piece being studied if none of his or her friends are playing it. This can be reason enough to give individualized repertoire to sensitive teen-age students.

So, what do we give the student at this point? The possibilities are infinite. First of all, the teacher must decide what is most important for the individual student. Will it be a short piece that can be quickly mastered, or is this the appropriate time for a larger ability-stretching project? Is there a specific technical area that needs development? Perhaps it is time to introduce music from a style or period that is not covered in the "Suzuki Violin School." Often the student will have a piece in mind that he or she has long wanted to play. Since the repertoire and order has been predetermined up to this point, now the opportunity presents itself to ask the student to suggest a few works from a wish list, one of which will often be appropriate. Of course, if the student's greatest desire is unrealistic, to play for example the "Concerto" by Brahms or Tchaikovsky, the teacher needs to point out that such a huge project at this point in development would take a very long time to accomplish. It is important not to suggest that Tchaikovsky and Brahms are forever inaccessible, thereby discouraging an eager student. Instead, suggest waiting for a time when the task will not be quite such a major project. Often a young violinist will have heard something like "Meditation" from "Thais" or the Monti "Czardas"; these are excellent interim choices and also honor the student's desires. Another option is to give the student two or three pieces from which to choose, allowing for a feeling of input but still enabling the teacher to retain control.

Many students at this point are ready to develop their lyrical and expressive style. While the Suzuki repertoire does include slow movements from Baroque concerti, often this would be a good time to introduce Romantic music represented by the Borowski "Adoration" and "Meditation" from "Thais." Also good choices are two arrangements of earlier works which are done in a more romantic style: the Paradis "Sicilenne" and the Veracini "Largo." If a larger work is appropriate, consider the Haydn "Concerto in G Major," the Nardini "Concerto in E Minor," or Viotti "Violin Concerto No. 23." To develop a virtuoso style and related techniques, consider "Allegro Brilliant" by Ten Have, or the famous Accolay "Concerto in A Minor." Some of the Fritz Kreisler pieces — "Tempo di Minuetto," "Liebeslied," "Schön Rosmarin" — can be very attractive and useful at this level. Other possible short pieces could include the Wieniawski "Obertass" or Severn's "Polish Dance." A bit more difficult, the Bartok "Roumanian Dances" are a perennial favorite. If a fine pianist is available, explore the Dvořák "Sonatina," Op. 100, or a Schubert sonatina. For experience with a 20th-century composer, consider the interesting "Sonatina" by Bartok. In other words, the violin repertoire offers many possibilities that can be motivating and can address specific technical or musical issues at the same time. Teachers should explore as much of this vast repertoire as possible and feel comfortable experimenting with new pieces. Public and university libraries, music stores, publishers' catalogues, and websites are all excellent sources of additional repertoire. In addition, many of the published collections of violin solos contain a wealth of material. Teachers should cover enough material at this level to be sure that the technique is solid, musicality is allowed to blossom, and the student is secure and comfortable before moving to the next level of difficulty.

As the student progresses beyond this level, concerto options could include DeBeriot "Violin Concerto No. 9," Kabalevsky "Concerto for Violin," Haydn "Violin Concerto in C Major," DeBeriot "Violin Concerto No. 7" — especially if the student is very young and needs more material before moving on — followed by Rode "Violin Concerto No. 7," and then Viotti "Violin Concerto No. 22." Bach "Violin Concerto in E Major" could also be used if another Baroque concerto is in order. Shorter works might include more difficult Kreisler pieces such as "Praeludium and Allegro," "Sicilienne and Rigaudon," Mozart's "Rondo," or "Variations on a Theme of Corelli." "Legende" by

Wieniawski is a great way to get into double stops. Smetana's "Aus der Heimat," especially No. 2, is a wonderful concert piece if a good pianist is available.

A special note is necessary regarding some of the literature composed by virtuoso violinists of the 19th century such as DeBeriot, Viotti, Rode, Spohr, and even Wieniawski and Vieuxtemps. Many of these works, with the exception of some compositions of Wieniawski and Vieuxtemps, are not currently in the repertoire of performing concert artists. Dr. Suzuki, in fact, made comments about not using many of them as he felt they were not of the highest artistic value. They do, however, represent a large body of the violin heritage and represent an era when performers wrote works for their own use that displayed their particular technical strengths and musical personalities. While these often charming compositions were never intended to be student works, they are highly idiomatic and make wonderful study material for young violinists to expand their technical equipment while learning to play with finesse and style. In addition, they are often highly attractive to students, and frequently meet them at just the appropriate emotional level.

If a Mozart concerto seems to be the thing to do next and the teacher is not sure that the student is ready to tackle "Violin Concerto No. 4" or "Violin Concerto No. 5," many like to introduce "Violin Concerto No. 3 in G Major" first. Another suggestion to explore would be "Violin Concerto No. 2 in D Major" or perhaps the lovely "Adagio," K. 261, paired with the "Rondo for Violin and Orchestra in C Major," K. 373, for these two shorter works are often more easily mastered than the famous concerti but still provide a wonderful introduction to Mozart's style.

Depending on the age and musical and technical maturity of the student, this might be the time to introduce individual movements from the solo "Sonatas and Partitas" by Bach. The "Allemande" from "Partita in D Minor" is a good place to start, followed by other of the dance movements such as the "Gigues" from the "Partita in D Minor" and "Partita in E Minor." The final movements of these three sonatas have great technical and musical value as teaching material. I would suggest that a significant number of these shorter movements be studied before attempting the first movements or the fugues from the sonatas. Some teachers like to precede study of unaccompanied Bach with some work from the Telemann "Fantasies," for many movements from these works provide an interesting introduction to unaccompanied polyphonic playing. If a student is eager to play the Bach "Chaconne" but is still far from ready for this giant work, the Bieber "Passaglia" may be satisfying, and provides good preparation.

Again, the teacher needs to assess each student's development continually, identifying areas that need strengthening, whether they are technical or musical. Additional repertoire should be sought out and studied to fill in any gaps before proceeding to more complicated music.

When the technique is secure and the musical understanding is ready for the challenge, a major concerto can now be introduced. Bruch "Violin Concerto No. 1 in G Minor" — especially the first movement — or Wieniawski "Violin Concerto No. 2 in D Minor" are good choices to begin this phase of development. The Lalo "Symphony Espagnole" is an excellent piece for technical growth; students can enjoy learning the first movement and perhaps two or three of the other movements, if not all five. The Saint-Saëns "Violin Concerto No. 3 in B Minor" might be the next step. Often the Mendelssohn "Violin Concerto in E Minor" is given as the first big piece of standard literature. If several other standard works are studied first, however, the resulting performance of the Mendelssohn will be more successful. The third movement is a good place to start, creating a good opportunity to make sure that the shifting technique is in fine order before attempting the first movement. Be aware that, if there is any weakness in this crucial area, few other works in the violin repertoire make such a public display of a deficiency as the first page of the Mendelssohn.

Clearly our repertoire does not consist only of concerti, so we need to be sure to include shorter pieces as well as selections from the rich sonata repertoire, especially if a fine pianist is available. Most of our students will rarely if ever have an opportunity to perform with orchestral accompaniment, so it is our duty to introduce them to other works that they can enjoy and perform for the rest of their lives.

From this point on, the wealth of material available for the violin provides much more than most of us can cover in one lifetime. Teachers should strive to create a broad repertoire for each student that includes many genre, styles, and periods of music. Sometimes by forcing the issue and assigning a piece that is not a particular student's favorite style, we can open new doors. Teachers also need to stretch themselves and constantly explore new teaching material. This way, both teacher and student continue to grow.

CHAPTER 18
REPERTOIRE

The following table contains suggestions for repertoire primarily for the student beyond Book Eight, although some pieces can be used much earlier. Some of the pieces, of course, will continue to be appropriate well beyond Book Eight. Concerti and sonatas from standard concert repertoire have been left out for the most part since these will be familiar to all. I have either used the following works for teaching purposes or I am familiar with their use by others. A few compositions have been included that were, unfortunately, out of print at the time of publication. Hopefully, they will become available again. If not, it would be well worth the effort to search them out at a large university or public library. If these resources do not produce the desired results, interlibrary loan services available via the internet make materials available, often in only days, from libraries all over the world. Publishers have not been included in this list since multiple editions may exist for a particular work. In this case teachers are advised to explore the options, keeping in mind what might be suitable for the individual student. It is hoped that this list will stimulate the teacher to investigate the rich and varied repertoire that exists for our instrument, much of which provides wonderful teaching material. Have fun!

UNACCOMPANIED SOLOS

Composer
Title
Comments

Bacewicz, G
Polish Caprice
An effective 20th-century work of moderate difficulty.

Bach, J. S.
6 Sonatas and Partitas
A mainstay of any violinist's repertoire. I suggest beginning with selected movements.

Prokofiev, S.
Sonata, Op. 115
Originally intended for group performance. Challenging, but appeals to some students.

Ribaupierre, M. de
Swiss Lullaby
A charming one-page work with simple double-stops and alpine flavor.

Telemann, G
12 Fantasies
Useful as preparation for unaccompanied Bach. Select individual movements.

VIOLIN AND PIANO

Accolay, J.
Concerto No. 1 in A Minor
An old standby for violinistic style.

Alard, D.
Brindisi Variations
A work in virtuoso style that teaches various violinistic techniques.

Bacewicz, G
Oberek
A highly rhythmical 20th-century work including double- and triple-stops, artificial harmonics, pizzicato chords, etc. Very effective and of moderate difficulty. Works well for group playing. This composer has many works for violin. Check listings of her music.

Bach, J. S.

Air on the G String [Wilhelmj]
> Great for getting around on the G string and a favorite for many performance situations

Aria: "Bist du bei mir" [Stamon]
> Good tone study and useful for church services, weddings, etc.

Arioso (Introduction to Cantata No. 156)
> Good tone study and useful for church services, weddings, etc.

Concerto No. 2 in E Major
> More difficult than the a minor but good for intonation study.

Jesu, Joy of Man's Desiring [Grace]
> Good tone study and useful for church services, weddings, etc.

Sheep May Safely Graze [Forbes]
> Good tone study and useful for church services, weddings, etc.

Bach/Gounod

Meditation (Ave Maria)
> The all-time best piece for developing vibrato. Good tone study and useful for church services, weddings, etc.

Bartok, B.

Roumanian Folk Dances [Szekely].
> Always a favorite with students. Good style contrast from the many baroque selections in "Suzuki Violin School"

Sonatina [Gertler]
> Similar in difficulty to "Roumanian Dances." Requires a good pianist.

Beach, A

La Captive, Op. 40 No.1
Berceuse, Op. 40 No. 2
Mazurka Op. 40 No. 3
> Charming pieces by this important female American composer.

Invocation Op. 55
> Another charming piece by this important female American composer.

Romance (1893)
> Beautiful lyrical romantic work, written for Maud Powell, the distinguished American violinist.

Beethoven, L. van

2 Romances, Op. 40 & 50

Favorites with many. G Major is often overlooked (contains double-stops.)

Beriot, C. de

Concerto No. 7 in G Major, Op. 76

Great technique builder, more difficult than the familiar No. 9, with more double-stops and bowing techniques.

Concerto No. 9 in A Minor, Op. 104

Great preparation for standard virtuoso concerti.

Scene de Ballet, Op. 100

Idiomatic and virtuoso techniques. Quite challenging.

Bloch, E.

Baal Shem (Three Pictures of Chassidic Life)

Wonderful concert pieces. No. 2 "Nigun" is especially popular.

Borowski, F.

Adoration

Great tone study.

Boulogne, Joseph
(Chevalier de Saint-George)

Concerto in G Major, Op.2 No. 1

A charming work by this 18th-century composer of African descent.

Brahms, J.

Hungarian Dances (Various arrangements)

Various arrangements available give a number of versions of these attractive idiomatic works ranging from simple to quite difficult.

Bruch, M.

Kol Nidre

Soulful lyrical piece, originally for cello but works well for violin.

Bull, O.

Saeterjentens Sondag ("The Herd Girl's Sunday")

Lyrical folk style melody by the Norwegian violinist who was a contemporary and perhaps sole competitor of Paganini.

Colridge-Taylor, S.

African Dances, Op.58

Attractive pieces, similar to Wieniawski mazurkas in difficulty and style by this violinist composer of African descent. (Check out several other works for violin and piano by this composer.)

Clebanoff

Millionaire's Hoedown

A favorite often used for performance by groups of advanced students.

Copland, A.

Hoe Down (From Rodeo)

A favorite with students. Virtually identical with 1st violin part in the orchestration of this familiar piece. (violin/piano reduction by the composer)

Waltz and Celebration (From Billy the Kid)

Another violin/piano reduction by the composer.

Corelli, A.

12 Sonatas, Op. 5

Good if more Baroque sonatas are needed. Select individual movements.

Dancla, C.

6 Airs Varies, Op. 89

Not too difficult introduction to Romantic violin style.

Debussy, C.

Beau Soir (Heifetz)

Lovely arrangement, notes not too difficult. Challenging to bring off the impressionistic style.

Desplanes, J.

Intrada [Nachez]

Beautiful lyrical piece arranged from an early work.

Donato, Anthony

"Precipitations"(1946)

Great example of mid 20th-century, with a number of interesting techniques. Very attractive and of moderate difficulty.

Drdla, F.

"Hummingbird"

Good for building finger dexterity.

Dvořak, A.

4 Romantic Pieces, Op. 75

Lovely pieces with some challenging double-stops.

Sonatina in G Major, Op. 100

Written for the composer's own children. This piece is an ideal introduction to duo playing with piano.

Elgar, E.
Salut D'amour
An old favorite that teaches a Romantic style.

Foss, L.
Three American Pieces
Very attractive pieces that are distinctly American in flavor. Rather difficult to do well.

Fauré, G.
Aprés un Rêve
A short piece in an impressionist style typical of the composer.

Berceuse
A short piece in an impressionist style typical of the composer.

Gluck, C.
Melodie [Kreisler]
A lovely arrangement of this beautiful melody. Great for working on lyricism.

Godard, B.
Berceuse from "Jocelyn"
An old favorite in operatic style with some brief cadenza-like passages.

Grieg, E.
Sonata No. 1 in F Major, Op. 8
A good choice as an introduction to the Romantic sonata literature. Requires a fine pianist.

Handel, G. F.
6 Sonatas
If more Baroque sonatas are needed.

Haydn, J.
Concerto No. 1 in C Major
Wonderful piece for expanding technique and musicality. Contains double-stop and bowing challenges. Various cadenzas are available.

Concerto No. 2 in G Major
A good choice after Book Eight. Good for developing lyricism. A number of cadenzas are available in a range of difficulty.

Hindemith, P.
Meditation from "Noblissima Visione"
A one page lyrical piece typical of the composer's harmonic style.

Jenkinson, E.

Elves Dance

A fun piece for children of very moderate difficulty. Good for sautillé.

Joplin, S.

Ragtime for Violin (6 Scott Joplin Rags) [I. Perlman]

Excellent arrangements with some challenging double-stops. Students love them.

Kabalevsky, D.

Concerto in C Major, Op. 48

Excellent study and concert piece for chromaticism and a 20th century style.

Improvisation, Op.21, No. 1

An attractive work in a 20th century idiom. Passage in octaves

Kreisler, F.

Andantino

Listed below are some of the many compositions and arrangements by Kreisler particularly suited to students at this level.

Chanson Louis XIII and Pavane (in the style of Couperin)
Liebesfreud
Liebeslied
The Old Refrain
Praeludium and Allegro
Rondino (in the style of Beethoven)
Schön Rosmarin
Sicilienne and Rigaudon (in the style of Francoeur)
Tempo di Minuetto
Variations on a Theme by Corelli

Kreutzer, R.

Concerto No. 13 in D Major

For students needing a challenging work for technical development prior to addressing the major repertoire. Contains many of the same technical challenges as the Beethoven Concerto.

LeClair, J.M.

Sonata in D Major

A Baroque sonata perhaps a bit more difficult than the Veracini E Minor Sonata. Contains some good double-stop work.

Mattheson, J

Air

A lovely piece arranged to be played on the G string. Great preparation for the Bach "Air for the G String."

Massenet, J.

Meditation from Thais

A favorite work that is often a wonderful vehicle for students to explore expressive playing while developing the techniques necessary for beautiful lyrical playing.

Miyagi, M.

Haru no Umi (Spring Sea)

A beautiful traditional Japanese piece that was a favorite of Dr. Suzuki.

Monti, V.

Csardas

A favorite with students and teachers that teaches idiomatic violin technique and style.

Mozart, W. A.

Adagio in E Major, K. 261

A beautiful piece that could be good preparation for studying a complete Mozart concerto.

Concerto No. 2 in D Major K. 211

A lovely lyrical work that deserves to be played more. Might be a good choice for a first Mozart concerto for study.

Concerto No. 3 in G Major, K. 216

A favorite and charming work. Due in part to the highly fragmented compositional technique used, a great deal of finesse is required for a successful performance.

Rondo in C Major, K. 373

A beautiful piece that could be good preparation for studying a complete Mozart concerto.

Rondo in G Major

A favorite Kreisler arrangement that is ideal for developing sautillé bowing.

Mlynarski, E.

Mazurka

A work of moderate difficulty that introduces violin style.

Nardini, P.

Concerto in E Minor

A late Baroque/early classical piece in a rather romantic arrangement that can be ideal following Book Eight.

Nero, P.

The Hot Canary

A "classic" that students love. Needs to be looked at as a point of departure for improvisation rather than to be taken literally note for note.

Novacek, O.

Moto Perpetuo

Challenging perpetual motion.

Paganini, N.

Sonatas, Op. 3 & 4 (orig. for guitar and violin)

Some of these could be a good choice for the student who wants to play Paganini but isn't ready for the more difficult works. Includes left-hand pizzicato as well as some rather challenging double-stops, etc. Great if a family member or friend plays guitar. The accompaniments are of moderate difficulty.

Cantabile in D

Beautiful Italian opera style. Neither double-stops nor the other technical issues of other pieces by this composer.

Paradies, M. T. von

Sicilienne

A lovely arrangement by this 18th-century woman who was reportedly a fine pianist and singer, as well as blind from childhood.

Piston, W.

Sonatina

Spirited work originally intended to be played with harpsichord but effective with piano. An example of a 20th-century work of moderate difficulty.

Previn, A.

Two Little Serenades

The first of these, especially, is a lovely lyrical piece in a contemporary idiom.

Potstock, W.

Souvenir de Sarasate (Fantasia Espagnole)

A character piece of moderate difficulty that emulates the style and techniques of Sarasate's Spanish dances.

Rachmaninoff, S.

Vocalise, Op. 34 No.14

Lovely lyrical piece. Can be effective played by a group.

Ries, Frz.

Perpetuum Mobile

Challenging, but excellent for developing fast fingers and sautillé bowing.

Rode, P.

Concerto No. 7 in A Minor, Op. 9

Excellent for developing style and bow control.

Sarasate, P.

Various pieces

Select according to advancement of player. Many are very difficult.

Schubert, Francois

The Bee (L'Abeille), Op. 13 no. 9

Excellent for developing finger dexterity.

Schubert, Franz

3 Sonatinas, Op. 137

Beautiful works that can be played at an earlier stage but require much finesse and control for a fine performance.

Ave Maria (various arrangements)

Useful for tone study as well as various performance situations. Octaves in the case of Wilhelmj arrangement.

Severn, E.

Polish Dance

An old favorite that students love.

Sinding, C.

Suite in A Minor, Op 10

Excellent for study and concert use. First movement is a perpetual motion, second is a beautiful lyric piece that stands alone, third movement contains many three- and four-note chords and could be good preparation for Bach fugues.

Smetana, B.

Aus der Heimat (Songs of Home) (moderato and andantino)

Two wonderful concert pieces, the second of which is an ideal work to precede major concerti. Requires a fine pianist.

Spohr, L.

Concerto No. 2 in D Minor, Op. 2
A good study piece that is not as difficult as some of the other Spohr concerti.

Concerto No.7 in E Minor Op.38
Difficult but excellent for framing the left hand (octaves etc.)

Still, W. G.

One can find a number of attractive concert pieces by this composer of African descent.

Stravinsky, I.

Berceuse [Dushkin]
Well-known melody from "The Firebird." Good for octave study.

Suzuki, S.

Prelude and Berceuse
A favorite of Dr. Suzuki for developing and demonstrating beautiful tone.

Svendsen, J.

Romance, Op. 26
A hauntingly beautiful concert piece. Composer provided orchestrations for full and string orchestra as well as piano reduction.

Szelenyi, I.

24 Easy Little Concert Pieces [Sandor]
Vol. 1 & 2   Not all that easy! Similar in character and difficulty to Bartok 44 Duets.

Tartini, G.

Sonata in G Minor (Didone Abbandonata)
A Baroque sonata with some good double-stop work. Urtext edition differs significantly from the more familiar Auer edition.

Variations on a Theme of Corelli [Kreisler]
A concert piece arranged from a few variations from Tartini's The Art of Bowing." Good preparation for Kreisler's "Praeludium and Allegro."

Tchaikovsky, P.

Serenade Melancholique, Op. 26
A beautiful concert piece requiring fine tone production. Passage in octaves.

3 Pieces Op.42
Three well-known works. Challenging.

Ten Have, W.

Allegro Brilliant, Op. 19
A favorite that students love.

Toselli, C

Serenade
An old favorite salon style piece.

Veracini, F.

Largo [M. Corti]
Beautiful arrangement of this lyrical piece. Useful for tone development and performance in a variety of settings.

Vieuxtemps. H

Cantilena
A florid lyrical piece with a contrasting middle section in 16th notes.

Viotti, G.

Concerto No. 22 in A Minor
The one Viotti concerto that remains in the concert repertoire. A great technique builder. Contains double-stops, right and left hand challenges.

Concerto No. 23 in G Major
Much less demanding than No. 22 but can be a good technique builder.

Vitali, G.

Chaconne in G Minor
Wonderful concert piece that offers opportunity to work on a number of bowing issues. Quite difficult. Several arrangements are available.

Vivaldi, A.

Concerti, Op. 8, Four Seasons
Always a favorite.

Sonata in A Major, Op. 2, No. 2
Effective Baroque sonata.

Wieniawski, H.

Dudziar (Mazurka) Op. 17
Virtuoso style of rather moderate difficulty.

Kujawiak (Mazurka)
Virtuoso style of rather moderate difficulty.

Legende, Op. 17
Beautiful lyrical work with double-stops of moderate difficulty.

Obertass (Mazurka), Op. 19, No. 1
Virtuoso style of rather moderate difficulty.

VIOLIN AND PIANO COLLECTIONS

37 Pieces You Like to Play (Schirmer)
This collection has been available for years and contains many classic solos, a number of which are listed separately above.

Barber, B.
Solos for Young Violinists Vol. 3-6
These volumes contain a number of the works listed above plus other attractive solos. CD recordings are available.

Gingold, J.
Solos for the Violin Player
A collection of attractive arrangements and original works of various periods, including a number not found in other sources.

Kreisler, Fritz
The Fritz Kreisler Collection, Vol. 1 & 2
These volumes include almost all of the familiar Kreisler transcriptions, original composition as well as a number of cadenzas.

Wen, E.
Masterpieces for Violin
An excellent collection of classic violin solos, many of virtuosic difficulty. A number of them have been out of print and are not available elsewhere.

Wier, A.
Violin Pieces the Whole World Plays
This collection has been available for years and contains many classic solos, a number of which are listed separately above.

CHAPTER 19
ARE WE SETTING OUR
STUDENTS UP FOR PAIN?

A 1986 survey by the International Conference of Symphony and Opera Musicians (ICSOM) found that 76 percent of those who responded suffered from a playing-related injury that caused absence from work. What, you may ask, does this have to do with Suzuki students and teachers? Actually, it has quite a bit to do with us. As we have more and younger players devoting more and more hours to practice, and learning increasingly challenging repertoire, we are seeing growing numbers of young students with injuries that relate to playing. Schools of music at the university level are seeing even more injuries among college students. These injuries that are caused by playing could have been prevented in many cases. As teachers we have a moral and professional obligation to learn as much as possible about the nature and possible prevention of such injuries. While we are not medical professionals, we can make use of certain known principles of body alignment and relaxation, and we can use some common sense, thereby preventing many repetitive-stress injuries. In other words, if bodies are used in the most relaxed manner possible with as little excess tension as possible, many injuries should be avoidable. (Susan Kempter's recently published volume, "How Muscles Work, Teaching the Violin with the Body in Mind," offers invaluable information for developing healthy playing habits from the beginning.) In addition, is it possible that teachers may be using unintentionally some teaching methods that contribute to injuries? Let us explore a few problem areas in which certain patterns appear.

One of the most common problems involves irritation to the tendons, muscles, and nerves in the left hand, arm, and shoulder. In many cases we can observe that players with these problems either play with a great deal of tension in the arm, neck, or shoulder, and/or are using much more finger pressure than necessary. In addition, sometimes the violin is being gripped more tightly than is necessary to hold the instrument. Such habits can be hard to break, since these students have usually been playing for many years and have had considerable time to develop bad habits as well as good ones. Teachers must slowly and carefully help students to retrain themselves. It is usually necessary to help the student discover exactly how much tension is needed either to hold the violin or to stop the strings.

Consider the violin hold first. A proper hold begins with good body alignment. This means that the feet will be evenly spaced under the hips with the shoulders directly above them. Caution must be exercised to be sure that the student is standing straight and that the torso is not twisted to the right or left. Placement of the feet is a crucial factor; teachers should be aware that the custom of placing the left foot forward with more weight on that foot will invariably cause the torso to twist. Over the years this can lead to back discomfort. Obviously the violin needs to be held securely enough to free the left hand, but many players also clamp down with the jaw or raise the shoulder to help hold the instrument. The result is excess tension. Experimentation with shoulder pads and chinrests can be of great help. While shoulder pads were once considered by many to be a crutch and therefore avoided, they are now used almost universally. At one time in history the same attitude reigned regarding the chin rest. How habits change! Many teachers discover what is comfortable for them, and then instruct or even insist that all of their students use the same. However, are all students the same height with the same jaw structure and neck length as the teacher? By analogy, do we all wear the same size shoes? Obviously we are different! Chin rests and shoulder pads must be just as carefully fitted to the individual as shoes, since they will be used for many hours just as shoes will walk many miles. Use caution with violinists who are tall or have long necks; the teacher often looks for ever higher shoulder pads. When the violin is raised overly high, however, tension in the right shoulder sometimes results from raising the bow up to reach the strings. This situation exemplifies how a problem on one side of the body can result from something happening on the other side. A higher chin rest, on the other hand, can be helpful. It is possible to raise a conventional chin rest by putting pieces of cork between the rest and the top of the violin, or by having a violin maker add wood between the rest and the cork that normally protects the top of the instrument. Chin rests in various models with adjustable height are available for purchase and can be quite helpful. A comfortable choice of equipment can be a great start to healthy playing.

Once the basic posture and violin hold are established, the left hand needs to be examined. Frequently the thumb is pressing excessively against the neck of the violin. In addition, the base of the first finger may also be gripping the neck. These two factors are sure signs of tension in the hand and arm. It is true that we must be sure every student develops adequate finger strength to be capable of clear articulation. In order to accomplish this we use various exercises in which the fingers pound the strings. Sometimes we even talk about hearing each finger strike the fingerboard. This is all fine and good up to a point. However, the fingers often continue to press into the fingerboard after striking, doing no good, but instead causing a high level of left-hand and arm tension. I have had success making students aware of their excessive pressure by asking them to play a note with the finger barely touching the string, as in playing a harmonic. Next, I have them gradually press the finger down until the note is stopped sufficiently to produce a clear tone when bowed. When I then ask, "Is this the amount of pressure you normally use while playing?," the response is invariably a surprised, "no."

Sometimes a tendency towards left-hand and arm tension seems to be related to the use of arm vibrato; some exercises to develop such a vibrato actually instruct the student to press the finger firmly into the string. In addition, many players exhibit a tendency to press harder as the music becomes more intense or if they want to emphasize a particular note. Great caution should be used when a student has these tendencies. As I have indicated, a teacher can demonstrate to the student the required degree of pressure, but it is quite another matter to retrain the individual to play this way all the time! My suggestion is to work very slowly and carefully to memorize the new feeling of playing with light fingers. The Suzuki student has the advantage of having committed a large repertoire to memory, so a teacher can easily pick old and familiar pieces such as "Perpetual Motion" or the second movement of Handel's "Sonata in F Major," and note how each finger should be carefully put down, note by note. Gradually, perhaps quite gradually, the tempo can be increased and the difficulty of the passage can be raised as the new habits of light fingers are established. At the beginning, these sessions should probably last only five minutes and increase in small increments.

It is imperative to keep reminding the student that this process is absolutely vital and will take time; it will take weeks, if not months. Musicians invariably become discouraged or depressed when they must call a temporary halt to the amount and level of playing, or when they must limit orchestral or other playing. The alternative may be more significant periods of time recuperating from injury. Teachers and parents must be supportive and keep reassuring students that this situation is only temporary, because players feel they will lose ground or perhaps never play again. To the contrary, my experience suggests that virtually all these injuries can be overcome, especially if great care is taken in the re-training process.

Let us now turn our attention to right-hand and arm injuries; these usually seem to be related to an excessively tight grip on the bow. Particular attention should be given to the thumb. Pressing too hard against the bow will cause tension, not only in the hand, but in the entire arm. In addition, excessive thumb pressure makes the hand inflexible so that bow changes and off-the-string bowings become difficult to execute. Besides the tension caused by too strong a bow hold, the right shoulder may also be raised excessively, leading to other eventual problems.

Injuries seem to occur most frequently when some change happens in the player's habits, or a new and stressful situation develops. This could be a change in technique or teacher, a new instrument, a new chin rest or shoulder pad, an increase in practice time, attendance at a summer institute or camp, or perhaps the added stress of preparing for an audition, competition, or performance. Sometimes injuries can be related to attempting large or difficult repertoire before the bodies of our young students are ready for such challenges. It may be unhealthy for a youngster to attempt the Tchaikovsky "Concerto," no matter how eager or capable the student may seem, until a greater reserve of experience and stamina is developed. Any of these factors, as well as others known or unknown, can trigger the onset of a problem. Remember that pain is the body's way of telling us something is wrong. We need to pay attention, look for the source, and deal with the situation. Too many times the young, or old, player thinks pain will go away, shows weakness, or worse yet, must be endured in order to play. This is not the case. Help should be sought if the pain continues for any period of time. If at all possible, seek the advice of a medical expert who has experience with or specializes in working with performers' problems. Such people exist. Remember that most doctors see very few if any musicians in their practices, and may have no experience with specific problems of musicians. Sometimes musicians are referred to sports-medicine specialists. These doctors may be helpful, but again, musicians' problems are much more specific in nature. Some musicians have found help working with alternative medicine practitioners such as massage therapists, chiropractors, acupuncturists, and so on. Be aware, however, that some alternative treatments have been known to cause more harm than good. The ideal situation may be a specialist in musicians' injuries working in tandem with a physical therapist, the teacher, and the student. An excellent resource is the book, "Playing (Less) Hurt" by Janet Horvath, a professional symphony orchestra cellist. This book gives descriptions of musicians' injuries; preventative measures such as suggestions for practice routines, stretching exercises, possible treatments, and regimens for recovery after injuries; and lists of medical professionals and clinics specializing in treatment of musicians' injuries. This book should be on every teacher's bookshelf and should be read before injuries occur. Another good reference in this regard is the book, "Athletic Musician – A Guide to Playing Without Pain" by Barbara Paull and Christine Harrison; Scarecrow Press, 1997.

As teachers, we have a moral and ethical responsibility to be on the watch for playing-related pain and injuries that our students report, and be prepared to direct them toward professional help. Most importantly, we must guide them to take at least a ten-minute break for each hour of practice, resisting the temptation to repeat a difficult shift or passage endlessly in one session. There is truly a point where enough is actually enough. We must also avoid assigning heavy repertoire before they are physically ready. The students may also be encouraged to vary repertoire within a practice session so they don't focus too much attention on difficult and physically-demanding pieces. A teacher must be on the outlook for excess physical tension and poor or unhealthy practice habits. Above all, we should avoid contributing to our students' pain.

CHAPTER 20
THE SUZUKI STUDENT
GOES TO COLLEGE

The time comes when the Suzuki student makes big decisions about how and where to continue education beyond high school. This involves much thought and consideration and is an exciting time for the young person, as well as a matter of much concern to parents. Many things should be considered. Is the institution large or small, public or private, and close to home or some distance away? How will it be financed? Will it require scholarships, loans, or second mortgages? Friends will make suggestions. There will be visits, interviews, ACT and/or SAT tests, and endless forms. This is a time of not only great anticipation, but also confusion and uncertainty. When the decision is finally reached, all will be greatly relieved.

For the music student, in particular, the college choice presents special considerations. First of all, the student must give serious thought to music's role during the college years. By the time college is considered, music will have been such an important part of life for so long that most students will be hooked, unable to imagine life without their instruments and the enjoyable times they share with friends in music-related activities. Fortunately, most colleges offer possibilities for further music study and participation in ensembles. At the same time, priorities should be established and specific investigation undertaken, for questions of concern to college music students are not the kind that glossy brochures or college-fair recruiters can answer. The student should find out from each institution, and its music department or school of music, if it offers what he or she needs and if those offerings are available in the type of program he or she desires. An on-site visit to the school being considered is probably more crucial for a music student than for a general student.

Many choices are available, whether the young musician is searching for a college, a university, or a conservatory. At one time the field was dominated by a small number of institutions. Besides the well-known conservatories, many state universities have now recognized that providing excellent training in the arts, specifically music, falls within their mission. They have developed excellent programs that provide not only the necessary courses, but also access to courses from other departments. In general, a conservatory places more emphasis on music courses, with minimal academic requirements. A university degree, in contrast, demands more academics along with the music requirements. Liberal arts colleges, while sometimes offering music degrees, provide an education that is diverse and requires more emphasis in areas other than music, therefore allowing less time to devote to one major area.

Many people will offer suggestions about which institution to attend. Family and friends typically rave about their alma maters, speaking of the "wonderful music program" at their schools. Sometimes this enthusiasm is based on a wonderful choir or an outstanding wind ensemble; be sure to investigate the string department specifically, since it is most relevant. Remember that many institutions do not have the necessary resources to be equally strong in every area. In addition, the student's current private teacher is an excellent source of information on prospective teachers, because he or she is aware of current possibilities and knows best who might be a good match for that student. Summer workshops, institutes, and camps offer wonderful opportunities for the student to study with different teachers and evaluate the comfort and stimulation of different working situations. Teachers with college or university affiliations are usually interested in recruiting a good incoming class and are eager to talk to prospective students. Do not hesitate to ask questions. Be careful of claims such as these: "If you come to study with me, I will make you into an international competition winner," "I will get you into a major orchestra," "I will launch you on a world-wide solo career." Such claims are actually unethical, since no one can control all the variables involved or predict just how a student's development will proceed. Visit the campuses under consideration, listen to some currently-enrolled students, attend an orchestra rehearsal, and above all, meet with the prospective studio teacher. An informal meeting and a trial lesson are great ideas. The student-teacher relationship will be a close one during the college years; it is vital that their personalities be compatible. This is also an ideal time to discuss the professor's style of teaching and the expected direction of the student's development.

If the young violinist is interested in teaching in the public schools, he or she will want to explore music education offerings. Colleges and universities invariably plan their music education courses to conform to the requirements for licensure for that state. Again, if possible, visit the schools under consideration and, in addition to meeting the private studio teacher, be sure to speak with a member of the music education faculty.

Suzuki students seem to fall into four distinct categories when making a college choice. The first group is made up of students who have played for many years, enjoyed positive experiences, made good friends, learned to love and appreciate music, but do not plan to participate in musical activities as part of their higher education. There is nothing wrong with this decision; parents and teachers must see this decision as something other than a failure, even in cases where the student has made wonderful progress with the instrument. We must remind ourselves of the initial reasons underlying music study. If we agree with Dr. Suzuki's philosophy, our goal is not to produce professional musicians, but to add a beautiful dimension to the child's life.

The second group includes the many students for whom music has been such a significant part of life that participation in college musical organizations is definitely part of the plan. Music, however, will not be his or her major area of study. Most colleges and universities offer a variety of opportunities for these musicians to continue playing. In many institutions both large and small, ensembles are open to all students, music majors and non-music majors. An audition is often required; if space is limited, music majors are usually given preference, since participation is required for music degrees. Moreover, larger schools frequently have a second orchestra that is open to all students on campus and may not even require an audition.

These groups are offered to serve the many students who want to continue playing, but with a somewhat lesser time and energy commitment. This may be exactly what students in the second group are looking for. As in all cases, it is strongly recommended that this student visit the school, meet the conductor, and hear the orchestra in either rehearsal or concert. This visit will enable the student to evaluate the group and determine if it matches his or her playing level. Some schools, especially small ones, lack the critical mass in their student bodies to support balanced instrumentation and a homogeneous level of playing.

Chamber music is another ensemble outlet that many Suzuki students have come to love. Fortunately for these students, small-ensemble coaching is a standard offering in most music departments. Again, an audition will probably be required for entrance and for appropriate placement in a group. Often, violinists outnumber the violists and cellists needed to form quartets. When violinists comprise the largest part of the population, a student with the ability to play viola may gain entrance to chamber groups or, in some cases, the school orchestra. Don't assume, however, that registering for a chamber group that meets regularly for rehearsals and coaching with a faculty member is the only way to play chamber music in college! Chamber music was written to be played in homes, or "chambers," and enjoyed by friends. For the college student, "home" can be the lounge of a dormitory or a room in the music department. The resourceful student will find friends in orchestra, put up a notice on bulletin boards, or walk the halls of the practice room area looking for willing participants to sight-read duets, trios, quartets, and quintets. Music should be available to these students in the music library.

The third group includes the student who wants to continue music study beyond an ensemble but not as a major area of study. There are two common solutions. One is to take applied violin lessons and possibly additional course work, even though the credits may not apply to the student's chosen degree program. The other is to select a minor in music. A music minor obviously requires less in-depth study than a music major. In addition to study of the instrument, there are typically music theory and music history requirements. A student is advised to take a careful look at the list of requirements to see if it satisfies his or her desire and if it is compatible with his or her major area of study. Scheduling often presents a problem when music is combined with another area, for large ensembles such as orchestra occupy great blocks of time and obviously are inflexible.

This leaves the fourth group: those individuals who want to make music their major area of study, most likely leading to a music career. To be successful, this student should be committed, highly dedicated, and motivated. This field of study is competitive and demanding. Hopefully, these students are musically and technically well prepared by their Suzuki backgrounds. At the college level, study will be even more intense, and the course load will be one of the most rigorous on campus.

Once again, care is vital in choosing a school. Be sure that the schools considered offer the type of training that fits the student's needs. Many possible career choices are open in the field of music. Performance in a symphony orchestra, chamber ensemble, or as a soloist may be the most obvious choice, but certainly not the only ones. Music education is the term used to refer to teaching in the schools; this career path requires special preparation. Also requiring specific training, music therapy is an exciting field in which music is used as a tool to bring about behavioral changes. In addition, music business and technology are fields that offer almost unlimited possibilities.

If performance is the goal, the student should be aware that the performing field is highly competitive, and that schools preparing students for this type of career are also competitive. Especially as a result of the enormous growth of interest in the Suzuki Method since the 1960's, there are many fine young violinists out there. They have started at early ages, receiving excellent instruction and making a commitment to serious study while still very young. Students who are interested in performing will do well to keep an open mind about exactly what they want to do. Many violinists combine orchestral playing with chamber music, commercial or studio work, solo performing, and private studio teaching. If private studio or college teaching is the goal, a performance degree is usually the first step. Another professional goal that offers special appeal to many students is Suzuki teaching! Preparation for this also often starts with a performance degree, although there are a number of options. Some colleges offer an undergraduate degree with an emphasis in Suzuki pedagogy, but teacher training in the Suzuki field is more frequently accomplished as part of a master's degree, or through summer workshops.

Combining areas of interest can open up many interesting avenues. Music business and music technology are two areas that seem to have career potential limited only by the individual's imagination. With such a career in mind, it would be good to visit the related department when examining prospective schools, for some schools have clearly outlined programs such as Music Business.

Sometimes a high school senior wants to major in music, but also explore another subject in greater depth in college. For this student almost all schools offer the possibility of a double major. These programs are demanding, frequently present scheduling problems, and often take at least five years to complete. Sometimes applied violin teachers discourage this course because they are afraid it will reduce the necessary practice time crucial in developing a fine violinist. My own feeling, on the contrary, is that each student should be allowed the opportunity to explore another area of interest. If and when the time comes to choose, that decision can be an educated one. Even if only one degree is completed, a choice can be made with open eyes and no regrets.

This is a word of advice to the high school student. While it is true that a great deal of the school's decision to accept a music student is based on the audition, it is not the only factor to be considered. A good academic record from high school is extremely important. In many cases, acceptance by the institution is required before an audition may be taken for the music department or school of music. The young violinist who desires a life in the music profession will need to develop fine organizational skills in order to balance music activities and academic study. If a student has poor grades from high school, he or she is considered a bad risk for higher education. College is more demanding than high school; a poor high school record suggests that this individual will fail even more in college classes. Sometimes private teachers tell their students the only thing that matters is how well they play, so time should be spent practicing rather than studying for academic classes. This simply is not true. The extremely rare but possible exception is a conservatory open only to a limited number of students.

Choosing the right school can be an exciting and awesome experience, with many possibilities and choices. Choose the one that offers what the student needs and the one that feels comfortable. Sometimes the choice is easy; sometimes it is obvious. Remember, however, that if the school choice turns out to be a mistake or if the student's priorities change, the choice need not be permanent. Many people graduate from an institution different from the one in which they started. Transferring to a different school in mid-degree is possible, common, and frequently transforming.

CHAPTER 21
PREPARING THE COLLEGE AUDITION

Now that a list of prospective schools exists, applications must be made, recommendation letters requested, and auditions prepared. The student should request the necessary application forms and read the directions carefully. He or she should make a schedule listing the necessary deadlines, complete the forms in a timely manner, and mail them early! For recommendation letters and references, students should ask teachers who are familiar with their work and who have a favorable impression of them. Provide these teachers with the forms the school provides, or supply a copy of the instructions along with the address to which the recommendation should be mailed. Inform letter-writers of the date the letter is due, and offer a stamped envelope. Give teachers plenty of time, as they often have many recommendations to write simultaneously. Do not forget to ask the current private teacher to write a recommendation, as well. This person knows the student and his or her current work better than anyone; failure to find this important letter in the file will make the examining committee wonder why it is absent! Never hesitate to ask private and school teachers to write recommendations as long as the student's work for them is of good quality. This is part of their jobs.

Now we will address the audition, itself! In truth, preparation for this important event must have begun prior to the application process. Find out the exact requirements for each school; usually they will be similar so that one may use the same material for all auditions. The most common requirements are: a movement of a standard concerto or similar work, a movement or two from an unaccompanied work by Bach, possibly a contemporary piece or an etude, scales, and sight-reading. Most auditions last only ten or fifteen minutes, so the committee probably will not have a chance to listen to everything that has been prepared. If a student considers a piece that does not fit the school's exact requirements, be sure to inquire well in advance if this choice is an acceptable substitute. Some schools are quite flexible in this matter; others are not. Some schools have a list of repertoire from which to choose. Sometimes the list indicates the level of material they expect, but other times it indicates the only works the committee wants to hear. Again, check with each school to avoid disappointment. After careful consultation with the current private teacher, pick pieces well in advance; nine months to one year is not unrealistic. Give serious consideration to using at least one piece that has been performed successfully before, so that everything is well polished and comfortable. This is a familiar concept for the Suzuki student who is used to performing an older, polished piece for recitals rather than the one most recently learned. The audition committee will not usually have a preconceived idea of one piece being more advanced than another. They will be more interested in how well the candidate plays than in what he or she plays. Choose repertoire that demonstrates strong points and will wear well for an extended period of time. Choose pieces that contrast tempo, style, and technique. Be sure to include one slow lyrical piece that displays beautiful tone, and another that is faster and more technical.

Often students and teachers think that a more difficult piece will be impressive to the committee. The committee will only be impressed, however, if the piece is played well. The object is to show what the student can do exceptionally well rather than to point out weak areas. For example, if the student has always had trouble with up-bow staccato, do not pick the first movement of the Wieniawski "Concerto in D Minor"! Prepare very carefully and perform the pieces as many times as possible prior to the auditions. Use them for recitals, other scheduled performances, or youth orchestra auditions; play them for family members and other students whenever an opportunity presents itself. In this way the student will enter the audition knowing he or she has already been successful with these pieces a number of times.

When it comes time to schedule the audition, check the desired date with the specific professor with whom the student hopes to study. He or she is undoubtedly busy, and may be unavailable on a specific date due to an out-of-town performance or master class. It is always a good idea to have the teacher of choice hear the student in person.

On the day of the audition, arrive in plenty of time to warm up at the site. A room will usually be provided for this purpose. Carefully warm up with some scales, arpeggios, and technical exercises. Go over special spots in the audition repertoire, but only very slowly and carefully. Avoid the tendency to rip through the audition pieces at breakneck speed; many have made this mistake, becoming overly excited and expending too much energy at this point. Some deep-breathing exercises or other relaxation techniques may be more helpful. Five or ten minutes before the scheduled audition time, the candidate should be outside the audition room in order to feel unrushed, and to be ready just in case the committee is running ahead of schedule.

When the time arrives to enter the room, the student should acknowledge the auditors with a smile and a greeting. If the committee is busy finishing up notes from the last performer, or has already listened to candidates for several hours, they may not be especially communicative. This should not be taken personally. They are only human, after all! Smile, anyway! When it is time to start, the candidate may be given his or her choice of work to play first. If so, the wise candidate will choose something especially comfortable. In most cases, a committee will not listen to a complete work, for there is simply not enough time. In addition, they are experienced at hearing auditions and will soon have a good grasp of the student's level. Normally the committee members will stop the player to request another selection. Again, they will usually only listen to a part of the work. If scales are required, choose a comfortable key, unless a specific key has been requested, and perform it with a slow tempo, perhaps one note per bow. This is a great opportunity to gain confidence. After the first scale, a faster tempo or a specific bowing such as spiccato is frequently requested. When committee members have heard enough they will inform the candidate, who may then leave. Thanking the committee would certainly be an appropriate gesture.

A word is in order regarding dress for the audition. Dress neatly and comfortably in clothes that allow for easy movement. Be careful of trendy styles such as bare midriffs and extreme necklines, but do not overcompensate by wearing jeans and sneakers. A formal gown or tuxedo is also uncalled for. I often say to my students, "Wear something your grandmother would like." Dress up and look presentable. The point is to look good and show respect for the situation, but not to leave the committee with a stronger memory of your attire than your playing!

The candidate will usually be informed of the results by mail. This can take some time, as there may be a wait for deliberations, or for an absent faculty member to hear and/or view the recorded audition. Sometimes other factors, such as the results of a music theory evaluation, will need to be considered. Notification of scholarship often comes at yet a later date.

Some schools will allow candidates who live a great distance away to audition via audio or videotape, and sometimes they will request CDs or DVDs. While it is greatly preferable to audition in person, it may be simply impossible. If it is necessary to send a pre-recorded audition, be sure to follow the school's directions exactly. For example, if videotape is requested, do not send audiotape because the student needs to make the best possible presentation in all respects, including how well he or she follows directions. Use the most current recording technology of the highest quality. High schools may have fine equipment available for this purpose, or a professional recording studio might be a good choice and well worth the investment. Use the best accompanist available and be sure the piano is in tune. Intonation makes a big difference! Allow plenty of time, perhaps even planning to record on more than one day, so that the best take can be selected. Failing to send the best demonstration of the student's playing will not be the kind of representation desired. Mail the tape well ahead of the due date, just in case there is a delay. Use mailing features such as delivery confirmation, return receipt request, package tracking numbers, and so on, so you can be sure that it has been received in time. Schools receive many tapes during audition season; as careful as everyone is, accidents do happen.

If all goes well and the student receives a letter of acceptance, everyone will be happy. Several letters of acceptance may arrive in the mail so that a choice will have to be made. If that is the case, be sure to read all the information carefully, and respond as soon as possible, certainly by the date requested. If the letter is not one of acceptance, there may be a number of reasons. Many schools can accept only a certain number of new students in a given year. There may be space for only a certain number of violinists in the orchestra, or the chosen teacher may have no openings in his or her studio. Of course, it is also possible that the applicant may not be equal to the level of students accepted by this particular school. Sometimes an explanation is offered, and sometimes not. In some cases a student will be invited to re-audition at a later date, with a contact name or number printed for further explanation or advising. A rejection may also indicate that this simply is not the best match of student to school. If that is the case, remember that many fine schools and fine teachers are available. Keep searching for the situation that fits!

CHAPTER 22
WISHING THE BEST
FOR A LIFETIME OF MUSIC

It is my fond hope that the suggestions in this volume have helped the reader "expand horizons." My intention is that teachers and parents will have gained some insights and ideas, and had their imaginations stimulated to work with students at an exciting time in their lives when so many new things are opening up for them. Hopefully, we can direct them towards the achievement of Shinichi Suzuki's goals, to which we committed ourselves when we began this journey with "Twinkle Variations." These goals are to develop each child to the highest of his or her abilities, and nurture that growth towards becoming beautiful human beings. If we have accomplished this, we have given them the gift of music, in whatever form and at whatever level they choose, to enjoy for a lifetime.